Convention COMEDIAN

STORIES AND WISDOM FROM TWO DECADES
OF CHICKEN DINNERS AND COMEDY CLUBS

By Jan McInnis

Cover design by Steve Dickenson
Book Design & Back Cover by Nikki Ward, Morrison Alley Design

First Printing 2014

ISBN 978-0-9840999-1-7

To my nieces and nephews, Alexandra, Ben, Brad, Drew, Patrick, Ryan, Abigail, Carrie, Noah, Saxon, Sanae, Katie, Tom and Sydnee. May your life be a fun journey with many great stories we can laugh at later!

TABLE OF CONTENTS

chapter one

Welcome to My World in Comedy

One of my most memorable moments, well before I got into comedy, was as a tour guide in Washington, D.C., during summers when I was home between college semesters. I was a great tour guide. I made up jokes and goofed around with the tourists, and I could remember all the city's facts and figures perfectly. There was another guide, however, a much older woman, let's just call her Agnes, who was not so on top of it. She was personable and sweet and you could tell she really loved her job, but she couldn't keep the facts straight to save her life. She'd point out the Air and Space Museum and call it the Mint, or tell 'em that the Jefferson memorial was named after George Jefferson from "The Jeffersons" TV show. OK, maybe I'm exaggerating, but I'm pretty sure, courtesy of Agnes, a lot of tourists left DC convinced that the president lives in the Capitol. (It's the White House for those of you who took her tour.) She was also constantly correcting herself during the tour until everyone on the bus was completely confused. She was the nicest woman, but she truly didn't know, or more likely didn't remember, her facts.

One day I picked up one of those guides to classes that you can take around the city, and I saw that Agnes was teaching a class on Washington, D.C., facts and figures. I was livid! This woman had a side business making extra money teaching people about stuff she couldn't keep straight! My tour guide friend Lauren was standing next to me and poor Lauren got an earful. I went off about how this woman could be teaching something that she herself was mixed up about and that the only way she could pull this off was by standing in front of the class reading the facts straight from a history book. She may be as old as the history she's teaching, but she still doesn't have a clue about it. I should be teaching that class! I was a top tour guide, and not only that, I was more entertaining! After my rant was over, Lauren calmly turned to me and simply said, "Well, Jan, she put the class together and you didn't."

In that instant I realized the difference between the people who "do" and the people who "rant." I could have come up with that class idea but I didn't, so Agnes gets to make that money and Agnes gets to tell those students any darn facts she feels like. I've remembered that lesson throughout my life and it has pushed me forward to *do* the things in life that I want to do instead of just rant when other people get to do them.

Comedy is so glamorous, or so I thought as I stood in the airplane bathroom cleaning off the vomit from the passenger behind me who had just gotten sick on me. She was air sick, as opposed to the flu. (I asked!) Twelve hours earlier I was onstage in front of hundreds of people looking like a big star. But the real stories are about what happens in between the great gigs, so enjoy your glimpse into the backstage of entertainment.

And it's funny how things turn out. Years later, I had forgotten most of my D.C. facts, but I jumped into a career that I loved but wasn't quite prepared for, and I became a comedian. Maybe Agnes and I had something in common after all.

Why Did I Write This Book?

I was terrified! It's 9:30 on a Thursday night in a little southern coal-mining town. I'm standing onstage in front of 200 slightly inebriated coal miners who are probably expecting some humor along the lines of "You might be a redneck if. . . ." The only problem is I am not Jeff Foxworthy. About 60 seconds into my act, I realize that it would be really helpful to actually *be* Jeff Foxworthy. I have *nothing* to say to them. I am out of appropriate material. And then . . . .

Welcome to my world and my book. Being a comedian is certainly a unique career, and when people find out what I do, aside from being shocked because I look more like a middle-aged mom than a hipster comedian, they always ask questions. How did you get into it? What's it like? Have you worked with anyone famous? Do you have another job where you make "real" money? And so on and so on.

So I wrote this book in part to answer those questions and give people a glimpse into the life of a making-her-entire-living-at-it comedian. I feel very fortunate to be doing a job I love that is also so interesting. It's the job I wanted to do as a kid, but I never figured I'd actually *do* it.

I wrote this book not only to tell stories about my experiences as a comedian but also to share some of the insights that I've acquired from my job. I get to be in front of thousands of people each year, in all sorts of situations, which has given me a fantastic education, far better than I could have gotten with 20 college degrees. And no, you don't have to be a comedian to learn from these stories. They are applicable regardless of what you do or who you are.

As a comedian, comedy writer and eventually a keynote speaker, I've been fortunate enough not to work in one industry my whole life, but rather to tool around the country sampling hundreds of different industries in ten times that many towns, interacting with thousands of people. All of this makes for some great learning.

I first cut my comedy chops in comedy clubs and then moved into the convention arena. I started out in comedy clubs because that's where comedians work. But I knew about the convention market because in my past life, the career I had prior to comedy, I was a marketing person, and so I occasionally hired entertainers for conventions. I saw that convention groups were more my audience: no late nights, not so many drunks and, better yet, no coal miners. (I'm not dissing coal miners. They just aren't my crowd.) So I aimed for the convention market and, through a lot of twists and turns plus some luck and serendipitous events (calling the wrong number and ending up talking to a guy who books corporate entertainers and who was looking for a female comedian), I got there! "I'm safe" or so I thought.

But the convention market brought a whole new set of challenges that had me once again on a steep learning curve. Comedy club owners are experts at putting together a great comedy show. They keep the room dark, so it's intimate. They shove the seats close together because laughter is contagious, and they make sure the stage is practically on top of the front row so that the comedian connects with the audience. You're set up to win in a comedy club. Plus the "anything goes" freeness of the club atmosphere is what most of us comics really treasure. Club owners, once they've hired you, pretty much leave you alone to do your act. As long as you're funny, you can get away with a variety of clean, dirty, edgy, angry or obnoxious humor. The crowd tends to expect the unknown, and for the most part, they don't get offended even when it's offensive because it's a comedy club.

Things are different in the convention market. And while the crowds were certainly more in sync with my humor, I still had some learning to do. The rules are different, the setups are different and the audiences are different. This isn't a bad thing, it is just, well, different. Things like the stage being on the other side of the dance floor, creating a huge moat between me and the audience, or being introduced after an hour-long lecture on healthcare reform (snore) became the norm. I've had a head table full of people seated *behind* me onstage and had a six-foot-tall chocolate fondue fountain arriving midway through my set. And those were the easy things.

But all these things—gigs gone bad, fantastic gigs, crazy bookers, fun people, weird hotel rooms and more—make my job really interesting, which makes for some great experiences and fun stories. And we comedians love telling stories.

Here are mine. . .

P.S. I have changed virtually all the dates, places, names and many other things, unless otherwise noted. What group I'm talking about isn't important. I'm focusing on the stories and lessons learned.

GLOSSARY OF TERMS

Gig – *A booking. I still call them gigs even if it's at a convention.*

One-Nighter – *A bar gig. Usually a gig in which the patrons don't realize there will be a show until the owner turns off the Monday Night Football game and sends the comic up.*

Killing – *Doing fantastic.*

Bombing and Dying – *The opposite of killing.*

Getting the Light – *In comedy clubs, there's an onstage light the comic can see. When it goes on, it means it's time to wrap up.*

Headliner – *Last act of the night in the club. Also called the "closer."*

Feature – *The middle act between headliner and emcee. Also called the "middle."*

Emcee – *First person on the show. Also called the "opener."*

Set – *Your act. "I did a set" means I performed somewhere.*

Break a Leg – *I have no idea. The only people who say this are audience members.*

Follow Someone – *Going onstage after another speaker or entertainer.*

Booker – *Person who books the club. They may or may not own it.*

Open Mike – *A show in which anyone can get onstage. The performers can be anyone from seasoned pros to totally brand new talent.*

chapter two

Finding the Funny in Failure

Now back to our story. I was terrified! It's 9:30 on a Thursday night in a little southern coal-mining town. I'm standing onstage in front of 200 slightly inebriated coal miners who are probably expecting some humor along the lines of "You might be a redneck if . . . ." The only problem is I am not Jeff Foxworthy. About 60 seconds into my act, I realize that it would be really helpful to actually be Jeff Foxworthy. I have *nothing* to say to this crowd. I am out of appropriate material. And then I start to sweat. We're not talking a little perspiration. We're talking rivers of flop sweat running down my back because I've got to fill another 29 minutes with comedy material that I don't have.

Or I should say, I had comedy material, but I realized that not one of my clean, well-crafted witty jokes about office cubicles or how I just hate going to the health spa is gonna work in this situation. I'm thinking, "Health spa? Really, Jan?" The flop sweat is not real attractive either, but looking fashionable is the least of my worries. The whole room is staring at me. And staring and staring. Then I realize they're not staring— they're *glaring*. These people aren't just unhappy. They hate me. Thirty minutes later, which seems like about 900 hours, I'm offstage and doing that "walk of shame" across the room. The door seems to always be on the other side.

And sadly, I'm not so concerned about bombing in front of these people or that they think I am the worst comic they've ever seen. What I'm really worried about is that I get paid. I've got a mortgage riding on this set. I didn't stay up on that stage to punish them or me. I stayed there because in the comedy world you have to "do your time" or the guy running the one-nighter will use it as an excuse not to pay you. My mortgage is depending on these guys laughing at my jokes about makeup and milk baths. Yeah, I know, this was not what I had planned for when I went into comedy!

"What are you going to do differently?"

That's what a veteran comedian asked me after one of my confidence-killing one-nighter bombs. "Because," he continued, "if you don't figure out what went wrong, then you didn't learn from it and you'll probably repeat it."

I'm starting out this book talking about failure because failure is the great equalizer. It brings everyone down to the same level, and people connect with it immediately because we've all been there. We've all failed at something. Of course the big difference for entertainers is that we have the pleasure of failing in a big public way in front of dozens, hundreds or even thousands of people . . . and even worse, sometimes in front of relatives! If you can stand being humiliated, then you have the makings of a great comedian.

But the old saying that we learn more from failure than success has held true for me. And following the advice of that comedian, I always try to take a hard look at these events so I can learn from them and, I hope, avoid such mishaps in the future. A failure story is ripe for review, evaluation and, when you put enough distance between you and it, humor. And while some of my fiascos admittedly were my fault and some are attributed to clients, I think that most of them are a hybrid of the two. The saying "it takes two to tango" certainly works to screw up a comedy show.

PMS at the Feminine Hygiene Party

I always talk to the client before a convention event so I can find out the scoop on the group and write some jokes specifically for them. It makes my comedy show more interesting to me, and it's a quick way to connect with the crowd if I start right off the bat with something about them. The industry-specific jokes I write are usually appreciated, but sometimes they get me in trouble.

Did you know there are whole industries built on things you've never heard of or given much thought to? It's fascinating. Take feminine hygiene products. There are companies that specialize in everything from wings, to pads, to the packaging. I did a comedy show for people who deal with one small aspect of these products *all month long* (I know, stupid pun), and their committee was a lot of fun; they had a sense of humor during our phone call. In fact, they were feeding me some information that I couldn't use because it was things like, "Oh, we make fun of a certain female VP's hair. Her hair is really big." I did have the good sense not to write jokes about her hair, but I was curious to see just how big this woman's hair was, especially since she wasn't in Texas.

As a result of our call, I came up with almost three pages of really hilarious show-stopper jokes. And no, they were not all about feminine hygiene products; only a couple jokes referenced that product. And by the way, I do have a clean comedy show, but if the group deals with something like

I was performing for a conference of mostly women, but there was one hip-looking young guy in the crowd. He looked like a fraternity boy fresh off the college campus. My show was rocking, and so I decided to play around with him. I tossed out a line that had something to do with him and dating; the whole group exploded into more laughter, but I noticed his face got very red. I knew something was up, and I felt bad. My suspicions were confirmed after the show when the client told me that it was really funny of me to joke around about dating with that guy because he's so conservative that he's probably never had a date. I felt even worse. I had used a stereotype of "cute college boy" to assume he was a player and had dozens of girlfriends. I resolved not to do that to anyone again and to stick with people I knew something about and that I was specifically allowed to joke with.

hemorrhoid cream, then I'm allowed to mention it in my show as long as it's reasonable and I don't go overboard.

I started out the show with 1,600 people in stitches instantly. OK, make that 1,599 people. Over to my left, at a front row table, sat the CEO, who did not look pleased. He had a sour expression on his face, like he just had eaten a lemon, and his arms were tightly crossed on his chest. At first I thought, "He can't hate the show. Everyone is cracking up!" But after about the fifth joke, I realized that there was nothing else in the room to get mad about but me. I positioned myself onstage so that the tall flower center piece was in our eye-line, thus obscuring his face. If I couldn't see his face, maybe it wouldn't unnerve me. No luck. I could still feel his gaze.

So a few more jokes in, I ditched the ones I'd written for the group and just went into my act.

Something was going on here, and I thought it best to go with my safe routine. The crowd was still loving it, but the damage with this CEO was done and so was I. After the show, he didn't so much as look in my direction for the rest of the presentations, and afterwards I didn't have a chance to speak to him because he fled the room.

Now, on the coal-miner-scale-of-failure that I just made up, with 1 being total epic fail like the coal-miner flop sweat and 10 being having the audience mildly irritated with me, I'd say this show was actually an 8 because people were laughing. Unfortunately, it was just not the one person who really mattered. The committee later told me that they loved the show but that their CEO was from another country, and while he spoke English, he did not understand American humor that pokes fun about his company. When he hired a comedian, his committee "got it" about joking around, but he had no idea this was going to happen. Lesson learned; get the CEO on board, especially if he doesn't understand the culture.

Failing in Front of Family

I think the worst bombing you can do is when the witnesses are related to you. Because they talk to other relatives and, well, you get the picture. Pretty soon, your bombing story is the highlight of the family reunion. When I started out, I had a lot of confidence, and consequently, I did a lot of stupid things. One of those was accepting a gig to fill a feature performer slot that required I do 30 minutes. And I would have had 30 minutes if every single joke I said hit. I was only doing emcee gigs at the time, where you have to do 10-15 minutes, and the feature money was way better than emcee money, so I took this gig. Hey, what did I have to lose? Apparently, a lot of self-respect.

My relatives showed up with friends to catch my show. They were looking for a good night of comedy. Well, they didn't exactly get that. I went onstage and proceeded to torpedo fast. And when you're new to the business, you don't even have the skills to bomb well. You get all sweaty and shaky, and you run through 25 minutes of material in about four. And not only did I have to contend with my dying act but there was a drunk woman in the room. Each time I hit a punchline, she would loudly and sarcastically laugh, "Ha, Ha, Ha." Of course the only way you could tell it was a punchline was because I paused, waiting for laughter, and since there wasn't any, all you could hear was her.

I wasn't good at doing "audience work" (deviating from my act by talking to people) in a room where the crowd didn't like me, but I knew that I needed to address it. So I finally looked in her direction and asked, "What's wrong over there?" In a dead silent room, she slurred very loudly but clearly, "You're not funny!" Ouch! I had nowhere to go with that one since I kind of agreed. Luckily it was near the end of my show, so I just mumbled something and got off the stage.

You know you did badly when, after the show, your relatives and their friends don't say a word about your performance. We all tried to pretend I had not just been onstage, and instead they started off with, "So, how's your family?" I did get some pity words from other audience members who thought the woman was out of line, but pitying the comedian is just as bad, or worse, than not laughing.

Later that night, I called my comedian friend Rob. Anyone who starts out in a new venture needs to have that one person whom they can call at any hour and cry on their shoulder. Rob Duffett was that person for me. I told him how humiliated I was that nothing worked, that some relatives were there and that I was in a dumpy hotel room with a huge bug crawling up the wall. He asked, "Do you have another show?" I said, "Yes, unfortunately, tomorrow night!" He said, "Good, because you get another chance." He pointed out that I could go back onstage and show that I've got a great act and that it would be way worse to run away and not get that chance. I calmed down and went to sleep . . . with the lights on because of that bug. And the next night went better. I didn't rock the room, but I actually got some laughs.

Of course a few years later, at a family event, those same relatives surfaced, and upon hearing that I was a full-time comedian, they mentioned that I didn't do so well when they saw me. I mumbled something about having gotten better, and then skulked away. First impressions are everything.

The "Wrong Fit" Failures

Occasionally I get a gig that confuses me because my act and the group's demographics don't seem to match. I wonder why this group would ever hire me, but they've presumably seen my tape and should know what I'm about, so I usually take the gig. That is how I found myself performing at a very nice dinner for about 40 people in a construction trade group. About 30 seconds into my show, I realized that they were not going to like my jokes. This was coal miners all over again, only in a convention dinner setting!

I got back to my seat feeling awful, and was kicking myself for taking the gig. Then, to pour salt in my wound, the president of the association leaned over and whispered, "These are contractors. You need to tell some d___ jokes!" Great. He wanted dirty humor. Ironically, I had followed their main speaker, whose keynote was all about how contractors need to change their image from being "good ole boys" who don't have much class. Apparently, somebody in the room wasn't listening to him. Two days later, I got a written apology from the association for their president's comment to me.

A few years later, I was in front of another construction group, not having a great set, only this time one of the guys yelled out something vulgar. That gave me a great opportunity to explain why I was telling clean jokes—it was in my contract. The group started asking me about this weird thing called "clean comedy," and they were amazed that I was "locked in" to doing it. Later, after I reported to the agent that it didn't go so well, he called me back and said that the CEO loved me! There was one person in the room who liked my act, and fortunately, this time it was the right person. Go figure.

Quitting

I once spent a week at a club in which I don't think I got two laughs each night. I was following an emcee who was local. He was very high energy and knew all the local references— bad restaurants, trashy neighborhoods, so he was absolutely killing. I was in the green room psyching myself out because I figured between his energy and his connection with the audience, I didn't have a chance; and with that attitude, I didn't. It was a long week. At the end of it, I was standing by the big bowl of comment cards, and I pulled out a fistful. Well, the first 20 said how awful I was, and many other things that pretty much assured that I wouldn't be booked there again. I thought about shoving those cards in my pocket, but then I figured if the first 20 said that, there's really not much chance that I just happened to pick up the only cards that skewered me. So I put them back. I was working the next week in a sister club to this one, and I figured with any luck, maybe the owner wouldn't read the cards until after that week was over, so I wouldn't get fired.

The next night I was doing a one-nighter before I started the week in the next club, and you guessed it, I bombed again! This was the last straw. I walked into the bathroom, looked in the mirror and started crying. I decided that I was done with comedy. I'd been gone from my day job for a little over two years, so I figured I could dust off my resume and get back out there. I just couldn't take the bombing anymore. Not only had I had an awful night and an awful week, but I'd experienced many one-nighters, including the

At The Punchline Comedy Club in Atlanta, over the door leading from the green room to the stage, a comedian has carved the words, "Make them come to you." Great advice for getting people into your act. A little lower on the door, another comedian has carved, "This room is great. If you bomb here, you suck. Get out of the business." So much for sage advice.

coal miners, that were crushing my self-esteem. I just couldn't take it anymore and decided that this next week was going to be my last week in this business. Since it was at the sister club, I was sure that they were going to hate me, too.

Well, sometimes things don't pan out the way we imagine them. The next night, I started out in the sister club, and I killed. I mean every word out of my mouth rocked. I think someone from above heard my promise in that bar bathroom, and the universe realized that I was serious about quitting comedy. I really had one of the most phenomenal weeks of my early career. And while I felt good about the shows, I was still too down from the past shows to notice, and up until the end of the week, I was pretty sure I was still going to quit comedy.

The headliner that week was very nice. He kept inviting me out after the show each night for drinks with him and his friends. He was struggling a bit during his set, and he said the problem was that this was his home club. A lot of people were coming out to see him and his act, but he was not doing his standard act. He was trying out a new persona, and so half of the people were coming out to see him, and half of them were coming out to see this character he'd invented called Larry the Cable Guy. Yeah, he got a little famous with that act shortly afterwards. The week I worked with him, I never took him up on his offer to hang out, but by the end of the week, I had decided to stay in comedy. Years later, I was performing at a theater in his home town and some guys came up after my show to say that "Larry" was their hunting buddy. He had told them that I was really funny and they should come see my act; it was very flattering, and a reminder that I'm glad I stuck with it.

Bombing With the Big Names

About five months into my comedy career, I got to work with a big star, D.L. Hughley. He was very popular and I was excited to be his emcee, that is, until I proceeded to have six horrifically bad shows that weekend. And by horrific I mean I got maybe five laughs total. I did so badly that the next time D.L. came through town, he brought his own emcee. Nobody tours with their own emcee! And in fact, the only time I ever heard this particular club owner laugh—he was a very serious guy—was when he called me about a month later and said, "Hey Jan, D.L. called; he wants you to emcee for him next week. Ha. Ha. Ha!" He thought my failure was hilarious.

D.L. is African American and his audiences were all African American. OK, there was one white guy at a show, who was trying to "fit in" with what he thought was the black culture. Every joke D.L. told, this guy would laugh really loudly and slap his leg like it was the most hilarious thing on the planet; he was embarrassing to everyone. After I bombed, he came over to "console" me, which only made me look worse, like we were together or something.

I'd never thought much about the differences in white and black audiences, but after that weekend I got to thinking that maybe my act wasn't suited for a predominately black crowd and I should avoid those rooms. Of course the minute you say you don't want something, you get all sorts of offers for just that thing. A couple weeks later, fresh from the D.L. failure, two of my open mike comic friends who were white invited me to join them at an open mike at an urban club. They said the club had an all-black audience, and that they got 300 people out to the show. Three hundred people would be my biggest crowd ever, but I declined. I said it's not my demographic. They kept at me because they knew that one thing us comics can't resist is a big crowd. After some more discussion, I relented.

True to form, that night there were 300 African American audience members, nine African American comedians, my two white friends and me. I wound up being slated for last on the show, which gave me all evening to think about how badly I was going to bomb. During the course of the night, every comedian ahead of me, except my two white friends, had a great show. Both of my friends bombed big, and were memorable because they were the worst ones on the show. I was getting more and more scared.

Finally, it was my turn. As I walked to the stage, I could feel the tension in the room, and everyone was dead silent; my knees were shaking and I was having flashbacks to my D.L. Hughley shows. I wondered if they were thinking, "Great, here comes another awful white comedian." When I finally got onstage, I was so nervous that I could hardly remember my opening line. So instead, I paused, looked slowly around the room, and blurted out the only thing that came to my head: "Well, I guess you all can't figure out who I came with?" The place exploded! They loved me. I had a wonderful show and ended up emceeing at that club for years.

I realized a couple things from those two shows. First of all, my two open-mike friends bombed because they weren't that funny, not because they were white. Secondly, I wasn't all that funny, which is why I bombed opening for D.L. at a professional show but was doing well in comparison to the comics at open mikes. Plus, I learned that when you're opening for a famous person, the audience doesn't care who the openers are. They pay big money to see the main act. When you put a new comic up there, then guess what? It annoys people. They wanted to see D.L., not this girl who wasn't very seasoned. It wasn't a skin color thing at all.

Covering My Butt

I once found an ingenious way to cover my bombing. I was emceeing for a week at a club, and the first show I did was awful. As the emcee, though, I'm supposed to not only tell jokes but also make the announcements and, at the end, encourage people to fill out the comment cards. Well, who the heck wants people to make comments on a show that you just stank in? Not me, so the first night I didn't say anything about the cards, and afterwards, the woman managing the room chastised me for some kind of dereliction of duty.

The next night was a repeat of my bombing, not announcing the cards and getting chastised. I asked the room manager what the big deal was about the cards, and she said she needed to give them to the club owner for the mailing list. She was under the gun and was getting pissed off at me; there was no way around this one. I had to announce those stupid cards. So on the third night (another bomb—shocker!), I came up with a brilliant plan. At the end of the show, I announced that they should fill out the comment cards, and then I added my own little spin. I emphasized that once they filled out their contact information, we were then going to call them and email them and call them again. I implied there would be a lot of hounding until they came back to another show.

I correctly figured out that if people heard how much we were going to bug them, they would surely not fill out the cards. But by announcing the cards, I had done my job. After the show, the manager didn't realize my ingenious stunt, but she was still panicked. She really needed to give the boss a mailing list of names from the week. I said, as honestly as I could muster, "I know. And you heard me really push those cards tonight. I just don't know what went wrong."

As we stood there talking about it, I had another brilliant idea, short of writing a new act overnight. I said, "Hey, I think people don't want to fill these cards out because it takes time. They've had a long night, and they're ready to go home. What if I just ask people to drop their business cards in the bucket, if they don't have time to fill out a comment card?" She loved it! The next night, when I bombed again, I was ready. I announced that they could fill out the comment cards in order to win a chance at tickets to another show or, emphasizing this option, if they were in too much of a rush, just drop their business cards in the bucket.

Did I mention how brilliant this idea was? We got a ton of business cards, hardly any comment cards, and the manager was thrilled. I was pretty happy, too! I finished out the week, bombs exploding with every show, and moved on, never to work that room again.

Now, I do try to be honest about my shows, and if that club owner or the room manager had asked me how I thought I was doing, I would have told them. But in that case, I didn't like the room and never wanted to work it again. And I didn't want negative comment cards about me floating around so the club owner would tell others about it, which might prejudice me with other clubs.

But I do my best to give an honest assessment of my shows. I once spent a week at a club in which the first show, the one that the club owner saw, went great. She then left town for the week and the next five shows stank. They stank so bad that during a break between the two shows on Friday night, I went back to my hotel room and changed my shirt. We comedians can be superstitious, and I figured maybe if I got rid of the bad energy from that shirt, I'd do better. Turns out it wasn't the shirt's fault.

For the last show of the week, the owner came back and the show went great. As she was paying me, she asked how my week went. I said, "Well, to be honest, I don't think I ever do very well in your room." She said, "I know, Jan. You don't do very well here. But I like your act, and I think you're very funny. So I'll keep booking you." I was shocked, but glad that I had fessed up. I continued to work for her and I did have some good weeks.

Moving Past Failure

When I started out in comedy, there were lots of us up-and-coming comics who used to get together to talk about our future and how cool it would be when we became rich and famous. Dreaming is always a key to any successful venture. But when you put your dreams in motion, such as actually getting onstage to do comedy, that's when reality sets in and you end up with weird, funny and frustrating stories that will fill a book.

One of the comics I used to hang out with started just as I did, working open mikes and getting bookings here and there. After a couple years, she started spending more of her time studying comedy and hanging out at the club rather than actually being onstage. She eventually faded out of comedy scene in my town and moved away. I ran into her during my travels and over dinner, after a couple of drinks,

I asked, "Why did you stop doing this? You were as good as me and you were getting work just as I did. What happened?" And without missing a beat, she said, "Because I saw what happened to you." She saw the hard gigs and the one-nighters and the drunk people and the bombing, and she got scared or disgusted or disenchanted or maybe overwhelmed by the task of going into comedy full-time. I said, "Yeah, but a lot of those hard gigs are over now. I've found my niche and I'm having fun." But it didn't matter to her.

I've told a few of my bombing stories here and I hope they didn't scare you away from taking on new adventures. I'm in an industry full of rejection. Sometimes it's a client or an agent or a TV talent scout who says, "No thanks, I'm not booking you." So being rejected onstage in front of lots of people has given me a solid foundation to be able to keep rolling with the punches for the past two decades. And I've always figured that if I can laugh through all of this public humiliation, then I've got a great defense when times get really tough.

I once got frustrated and thought, "When am I going to stop bombing?" and my next thought was, "When I stop doing comedy." Thankfully the bombings are few and far between now, but the ability to handle hard gigs has served me well in my career, as you'll see in the following chapters.

WISDOM

Be careful when you do something just for ego or money.
Some of my failures can be attributed to my wanting to move up the comedy ladder when I wasn't ready or my taking a gig for the better money. I let my "wants" get in the way of my "shoulds" and it resulted in a bad show.

Dig deeper.
Don't take things at face value; many times, there's something going on behind the scenes that you don't know about that is the *real* cause of a failed venture, as in the D.L. event. And at the hygiene event, if I had dug just a little deeper, I could've avoided the problem all together. The committee was feeding me information on subjects that I knew I couldn't make fun of (a VP's hair). That should have been a red flag for me to make sure it was okay with management to joke about their company.

Do it your way even it means failing.
Sometimes I bombed because the group wanted dirtier humor. Had I decided to write dirty jokes to accommodate, I would not be proud of my act, and I probably wouldn't have moved into the convention market so easily. Stick to your guns and know yourself and your goals; you'll eventually wind up where you want to be.

Don't give failure too much energy.
When I focused on my failures too much, I almost quit the business. And my friend didn't go into comedy because she focused on my failures. Don't keep hashing over what didn't work or you'll screw up your shot at success.

Take the opportunity to make things right.
Rob's advice was great, and going back on stage the next night after failing in front of relatives was the best thing I could've done. And when I was honest about not doing so well at a club, I actually wound up with a compliment!

chapter three

You Want Me to Perform Where?

Comedy is one of the easiest forms of entertainment, if it's done right. All you need is a microphone, a stage, lighting and a focused audience. But have one of those things out of kilter, and you get a different experience.

My goal when I started out working in tough one-nighters was to get so successful that I'd never again have to perform in a room in which you can hear the blender! Bartenders seem to have great timing. They always crank it up right as you're hitting a punchline. No one hears you and you look foolish. Little did I know that there are room setups that a make the blender gigs look easy.

Swirling Around

I once got to do comedy at a company party on a turntable, or lazy Susan for those of you over 50. The room was stationary, but the part of the floor that I performed on spun around, making a 360-degree lap every 10 minutes, so in a 60-minute show, everyone got to see my face six times. There was a wall behind me, so people on each side of the room couldn't see each other, which made it even more interesting because I'd spin slowly into one part of the room, annoy the people who had forgotten there was comedy, and then I'd spin out. Sixty minutes of this. The client was drunk when I got there, so she didn't see the problem. She probably was drunk when she reserved a spinning stage and a comedian, but I can't say for sure. My only saving grace was that the DJ was booked through the same agency, so I had a witness to this mess. Needless to say, my comedy-on-a-turntable did not resonate well with the group.

I got another chance to spin at an event a few years later, but this time, instead of the floor spinning, it was just me! The company that hired me said that since there would be more than 1,000 people in attendance, they wanted to make sure everyone could see me. So they put me on a pedestal in the middle of the room, with people sitting all around me, and asked me to spin while I told jokes. I've always wanted to be put on a pedestal—figuratively, not literally. I didn't know about the spinning until I arrived at the event, and the client kept asking me before the show, "So do you think this is OK?" I refused to say yes because I didn't want to take the blame for it, so I just responded, "I'll try it." I did end up having a lot of fun with it, and even though the show went very well, I would not recommend spinning comedy. This is when I decided that being famous would really, really come in handy because I could put my foot down and demand that I not spin. But I needed the money and I'm not famous, so spin I did.

Static and Still Dreadful

Of course there are stationary room setups that are not conducive to comedy either. Try telling jokes in the basement ballroom of a fancy hotel with posts placed throughout the room. I started off trying to dodge in between them and around them and beside them, until I finally blurted out, "I went to college so I didn't have to get a job dancing around a pole!" It got a big laugh and I got to acknowledge the situation I was in. At least everyone in the room was experiencing my "pole dance," so it was funny and the show still rocked!

On several other occasions I've been booked to do comedy in a situation in which part of the audience was not in the room. But how can I perform live comedy when some of the audience is

I love to take a tour of the companies I'm hired to entertain for. Some of the cool places I've seen include:

- *Little Debbie Snack Cake plant, where any employee can take a hot snack cake off the conveyor belt.*

- *The Hanford site where the first atomic bomb was made.*

- *A women's prison where they also train service and guide dogs.*

- *The pro bowler's bowling alley in Reno, Nevada.*

not in the room? Well, no worries, say the clients, because I would be on a speaker or, in some cases a speaker and TV monitor, so people can hear the jokes, you know, like radio if it were live. Well, you know what I learned? It really doesn't matter which one—speaker or speaker plus video—because if the whole audience isn't in the room, it is a crappy setup. I did this once on a boat cruising on a lake. I was broadcast throughout the entire boat, but there were seats for maybe 30 people in the room where I was performing. The 30 people liked me. To this day, I have no idea if the other 150 people were even listening.

> *I was performing for 800 people and I noticed that the right side of the convention center was laughing and the left side was silent. Ten minutes into my show I got a tap on my foot. The client was at the foot of the stage. She whispered loudly, "They told us before the event that the speakers on the left side of the center don't work!"*

One key if you're going to have people watching the comedian on a monitor, instead of live, is to have the comedian actually on the monitor. One company that had me perform in a bar at their company function tried this but, for starters, the bar was long and narrow, and I wasn't on a riser, so only the seven people in the front could see me. Strike one. And not all the monitors were showing me; some were still broadcasting the football game. Strike two. Oh, and the camera was on the wall to my right, *not in front of me*! For anyone to see my face, I had to face the wall and do comedy with the audience to my left. Strike three! All we needed were locusts swarming to have a full-on disaster that qualified for FEMA relief! Actually, locusts might have been helpful, as they would have grabbed people's attention.

Another one of these "split-the-audience-up-so-the-comic-can't-see-them-all" setups was at a one-nighter, in which there was a glass wall and speakers broadcasting on the other side of the wall. I could at least see the people in the other room ignoring me. But for those who were laughing, all I could see was their heads bobbing. The glass wall created a sound barrier. There was also a window behind the audience, and when I looked over the people playing pool (no, they didn't stop their game for my show) into the parking lot, I could see my car. I did my entire set staring at my car. When I got off stage, I walked straight to it, got in and squealed tires out of the parking lot.

And sometimes, the stage is a little more makeshift than I'd like. I did a show at a college, during lunchtime, in which I had to stand on a long, narrow lunch table. These college gigs are called "nooners" because they happen at noon in the cafeteria. Many comedians do them and the comedy-on-a-tabletop is pretty standard. Weird. I don't know how many decibels the noise level got to that day, but I'm pretty sure no one heard my jokes; the students were more interested in their burgers and fries than my humor. But no one questioned why an almost 40-something woman was standing in their cafeteria on a table. I did my act to the clock. When it struck 45 minutes, I jumped down and left. I now do a lot of events for healthcare groups, and they have a term "never-event" for a mistake that should have never happened, like operating on the wrong body part or injecting the wrong medication. I think that term, never-event, sums up these nooners.

In addition to these venues, just a few other off-the-wall comedy settings I've told jokes in include:

- in a bakery

- on a gigantic bowling alley with people inside gigantic clear bowling balls rolling by me

- in a winery

- outside in a field next to a canal with huge barges going by

- on a floating dock on a lake with the audience on the grass embankment on shore

- at a restaurant while people were eating (I was told the wait staff as well as the audience loved me!)

- at a restaurant filled with hundreds of statues

- in a multimillion-dollar gymnasium with a $20 sound system

- on an aircraft carrier with the wall open behind me so you could see the ocean (I was told, "Get off stage when you hear the fireworks starting.")

- inside a museum, on the steps leading to an exhibit

And all these events went well. OK, the $20 sound system was a challenge, but I'd prefer to just have a standard stage, thank you. Unless you put something weird on the stage, which brings me to . . .

Lecterns I Have Known and Other Junk on the Stage

Do you see a lectern in front of the comedians on Comedy Central? No? Well, did you ever think there was a reason why comedy isn't done behind one? There is. Lecterns are generally a sign that the speaker is going to be really, really, really boring. Pull out your phones and start catching up on email, because this talk is going to be a snoozer. Yet, the number of clients at conferences who have tried to get me to do stand-up comedy behind a lectern is *a lot*. Only two have been successful. And guess what happened both those times? The show was less than perfect. Lecterns are for people to clutch when they're afraid of the crowd or to put notes on when they haven't a clue what their speech is about. Lecterns are not for comedy. We comedians need to be in front of the crowd so that we can connect with them and they with us.

At one of my lectern comedy events, the main cast of characters ("big wigs," if you will) had all of us at a head table with the lectern in the middle and the audience in front of us. So I had people sitting right beside me on both sides as I did my act. Thankfully, I was given a handheld microphone, but I still had to stand behind the lectern or no one would see me. Guess how well that show went? On a scale of 10 to "in the toilet," you would be right if you guessed "in the toilet."

I was once collecting my pay in the office of a comedy club, which was in the rafters of the club and had a really low ceiling, like two inches above my head. As I was getting paid, I heard running around above me, only to be informed that those were rats. If I hadn't needed the money so bad, I would've run screaming from the place.

The next worse thing after having me stand behind a lectern is to have people at a head table behind me while I perform on an island between them and the audience. I'm guessing the head table people wanted to let everyone know how important they were by refusing to sit with the masses. Boy, I hope I combed the back of my hair. It is unnerving to have people behind you while doing comedy because you hope they are laughing and not checking their cell phones.

Decorations Are the Devil

I know that sounds mean, and really, decorations can be beautiful if done right, but they are the devil if they're not. And have I had to work through a lot of weird (read distracting) decorations! The committee wants big, voluptuous flowers cascading down a fountain of beauty, right smack in the center of the table and towering over the guests. We comedians just want to be seen. I'm 5'10", but even on a stage I've still been dwarfed by some incredible centerpieces.

And sometimes the decorations are stealthy and creep up on you when you least expect it. During one event, I was having a fantastic show. I had jokes about their silent auction items, jokes about the group and jokes from my act. All were hitting, until the last 10 minutes. Then people stopped laughing and there was a murmur in the crowd along with what comedians dread most: *silence*. Because of the blinding spotlights, I needed a dog or a cane to even find the edge of the stage, so I had no idea what was happening out there. But I kept going along until I'd done my time.

When I got off stage, the client said, and I'm not joking, "I guess I shouldn't have pushed in the six-foot-high chocolate fondue fountain during your show." No, maybe that wasn't the best idea in the world because *nothing* can compete with chocolate. You could be announcing that we found life on Mars or that the Surgeon General has OK'd a pill that will make you instantly drop 30 pounds, and guess what? No one will listen to you if they're distracted by free chocolate. I know it's bad for my waistline, but I didn't realize how deadly it could be for my comedy.

Clearing Dishes and People Eating

Back during my junior high school days, I was in charge of "joke of the day" at our lunch table. I had to come up with a joke, original or not, for each day and share it with my lunch mates. My crowning achievement was when I got one of my friends to laugh so hard that she spit out chocolate milk through her nose. I can't remember the joke, but I was very, very proud, even though I was covered in chocolate milk. But I learned that telling jokes while people are eating only works when you're in junior high school, not so much when you're in front of a convention crowd.

I've had to entertain on a few occasions in which people had just started eating, and, well, people can't laugh with a mouth full of chicken. It's not that I bomb at these events, I just can't really tell how well I'm doing. After the show people will say they liked it, but what I need is feedback during the show. And I always have that seesaw going on in my head: Which material do I burn while I'm waiting for them to finish eating? The killer opening lines in my act, the jokes I wrote specifically for the group, or the weaker material I've stuffed in the middle. I've decided that it doesn't matter. I'm not going to get much reaction to any of it. As one audience member put it, "I could tell people were finishing lunch because you started getting laughs."

Another big distraction I've found that can hinder a show is having a break in the middle. Like people are going to laugh so much, that they have to stop 30 minutes in so they can catch their breath and go to the bathroom. Comedy clubs have a formula for a successful show, and one of those ingredients is that comedy builds. That's why there's no break between the emcee and the headliner. One group had me do 30 minutes of material, then I sat down and we had dessert, and then I went back up and did the other 30 minutes. The show went well, but it was odd and, really, what do I start the second half with? "Hey remember me? How was that dessert? Whew! Glad we had that break. OK, so I was talking about kids . . . ." I guess it could only be worse by having a break to eat chocolate fondue.

Wrap All These Distractions Up into One Venue, and You Have . . .

Exhibit halls! It turns out that exhibit halls really should be used only for networking, not comedy shows. How do I know this? You guessed it; I've been booked to do comedy in exhibit halls, and they've got all of these bad setups in one convenient place—distracted people, large in-your-way decorations, a bad sound system and a hidden location in which to stash the comedian. TA-DA! It's the epitome of awful venues.

The speaker system in an exhibit hall is barely conducive to announcing raffle winners. Trying to listen to a comedian and follow her jokes all the way from setup to punchline is impossible. Couple that with people tearing down booths and walking around visiting booths, and you've got the trifecta for a tough event. I did a gig at a home show once where I was stuffed away in a corner of the hall, and they were making announcements over my show. My show went a little like:

Me: "So I'm on a diet, and I tried yoga."

Loudspeaker: "Attention everyone! Don't miss the demonstration of our veggie food processor. Aisle 25.

Me: "I can't do yoga because . . ."

Loudspeaker: "We'll be drawing raffle tickets for a complete bathroom makeover. Get rid of that ugly toilet now!"

Me: "No, it's not because of the bathroom makeover. I can't do yoga because . . ."

Loudspeaker: "Free cookies on aisle 16!"

You get the picture. I lost a good portion of my female audience with the announcement that a big TV soap opera star was signing autographs in booth 1467. And I have to think the people who weren't sitting at my show—the ones visiting the booths—were just as confused because I was being broadcast throughout the exhibit hall. They probably wanted to enter to win the bathroom makeover, but instead they're listening to some woman tell them about yoga!

Turns out I did have a captive audience . . . of guys whose wives had dragged them to the expo. They *loved* me and were not in the least bit lured away by half-price jewelry. Plus, toward the end of my show, the school kids who were performing on my stage next arrived. All 30 of them, right down the center aisle so they could sit up front and be ready. It was incredibly distracting, but at least my audience doubled because their parents showed up too! Afterwards several of the husbands bought books and commented about how good I was, like they couldn't believe I was so good and yet I was performing at this venue. Me neither.

WISDOM

Don't overthink things.
Some of these situations came about because the client was overthinking the audience, such as, "Comedy will make the students eat lunch." No, hunger will make the students eat lunch, but the client was trying to fix something that didn't need fixing. Trying to get too creative and stuff too many things into a situation, like a comedian and huge decorations, lecterns and exhibits will make your head spin, even if you're not telling jokes on a lazy Susan!

Relax and experience everything.
When I can't change a situation, then I try to stay really present so that I can experience it fully. That's what life is about for me; different experiences. And anyway, when else am I going to float around on a lake telling jokes while my audience sits on shore?

chapter four

She Better Be Funny or We're Not Paying Her . . . and Other Great Introductions

I've had quiet introductions and noisy introductions, drunken introductions, people-trying-to-be-funny-but-weren't introductions, long introductions, last-minute introductions and no introduction. One woman even introduced me by saying, "She better be funny or we're not paying her." I was funny and I did get paid. Whew!

Considering some of the things that have been said before my going onstage, it's a wonder I have any good shows. The introduction might be one of the most important things you can do to help the comedian be successful. It should set the mood, but many times it is a last-minute, off-the-cuff sort of thing. I've shown up on several occasions to double-check with the client and found out that they did not bring my introduction. That's an easy fix because I can give it to them. The harder fix is when they improvise, like the woman who thought she was being funny by making a comment about not paying me.

Long, Boring and Incorrect

The long introduction, in which they've swapped my bio for my introduction, is

> *Rob Duffett didn't want the audience to know he was a lawyer, so he had an introduction that he insisted everyone use: "Please help me welcome the 1976 Pine Wood Derby Champion... Rob Duffett."*

probably the most common mistake. I've done a lot of cool things. I've written for everyone from "The Tonight Show" to guests on "The Jerry Springer Show." (My parents are so proud.) I've been featured in prestigious newspapers, such as *The Washington Post* and *The Wall Street Journal*, and in more than 20 years of doing this comedy thing, I have some interesting credits. But for crying out loud, we don't need to tell the audience all about it right before I go on. That's why I put it in the bio, not the intro. My bio is 10 minutes of interesting reading if you're my mom. She loves to hear all that I've accomplished. The audience is another story. In one case, the person didn't read my bio, she read the marketing email that I had sent to her to get the gig! She introduced me by telling the audience about all my keynotes so that I could be considered as a keynote speaker for her conference. That was awkward.

On several occasions, the introducer actually read some of my jokes, which made the jokes lose a little something when I told 'em. The introducer is killing with 'em and I'm backstage trying to figure out how to follow myself. And speaking of stealing my jokes, I once did a string of shows for the same group, and on the third day of shows, one of the clients told me that during his breakout session, he used one of my jokes because "it fit perfectly." Great, I'm glad he was successful

I once did a one-nighter in which the group was waiting on union election results. They were on the other side of the bar ignoring the show, and the people at the bar had their backs turned to the stage. The headliner came in, saw the setup and went back out to his car. He thought I would bail early and make him do the whole show. I didn't, but I got off at the stroke of 30 minutes. The headliner did his entire show with his back to the crowd since they had their back to us.

with my act. The guy happened to be Russian, so that night when I did the joke and nobody laughed, I said, "That joke is much funnier if X hadn't done it in his session. I guess X is a Russian name that means 'thief.'"

I've also had nervous people introduce me, and that's usually OK, sometimes even comical. One guy was very anxious, but he still didn't bring notes with him. All he could remember about me was that I had freelanced for a major entertainment outlet ("The Tonight Show"), and so in his nervousness he blurted out, "She's a writer for *Reader's Digest*." Great, the audience is probably thinking, "How hard is that? Don't they solicit articles from *anyone*?" That introduction still cracks me up, and one of my comic friends said he wanted to go out after me and clarify: "She's a reader for *Writers Digest*."

I'm used to people screwing up my name too, but I have a hard time when they mix up my title. My website is www.TheWorkLady.com, and I started out going by "The Work Lady" for two reasons. One was that no one knew how to spell my last name, so I wanted to find something easily searchable, and the second was because I did a lot of work humor. Well, "The Work Lady" is all good and fine except for the dozen or so times that I've been introduced as "The Working Girl." That's a different profession, though I'd still be staying in a lot of hotels, just not the fancy ones. The audience generally looks a little curious about the kind of entertainer who was hired, while I walk onstage trying to decide if I should spend a minute to correct the client, or just let people think I'm the most unsexy "working girl" they've ever seen.

Some people give me quiet introductions. They don't mean to; they just don't know how to use a microphone, so they stand 30 feet away from it or hold it down at their waist. Someday I'm going to snap and crawl across the stage and push the mike up to someone's mouth. Or occasionally the crowd is so loud that the poor introducer can't get them to be quiet, so instead of flashing the lights off and on or whistling, they just introduce me and let me deal with the loudness. This leads to my opening with, "HELLOOOOOO. Hey you guys. HELLOOOO." Not real funny. There's also the other extreme, in which I've had the introducer not be able to get them quiet so he yells at them, "Shut up because we've got a comedian coming up!" Yeah, now that we've all been publicly chastised, let's laugh. I just became the annoying entertainment that interrupted their conversations.

And some introducers want to be comedians themselves, so they insert humor into my intro. If their attempt at humor is not funny, it reflects badly on me. The audience thinks I wrote that crappy line for them to say. And even if it's funny, it might not be right. I worked at one comedy club in which the owner wanted to be a comedian, but he was an owner. So he emceed the show by going up ahead of us and doing close to an hour of comedy material; material I think he "borrowed" from the comedians who worked his club. By the time I'd get to the stage, he'd tell me to cut my act down to 20 minutes because we were running short of time. Hmm, I wonder how that could've happened.

And once in a while, I've had people start the introduction with, "Is she in the room?" This is after I've already introduced myself to them and told them I'm ready to go whenever they

One night during the middle of a show that was going very well, a young couple got up and stormed out. I started worrying, "What did I say to piss them off?" Afterwards, one of the waitresses said she saw them at the ticket counter demanding their money back, and the girl said, "This show isn't that funny anyway." I felt awful, so the waitress went to the box office to find out more, and she returned laughing. It turns out the young couple was younger than I thought. In fact, the girl was not old enough to drink alcohol. When another waitress carded her, the girl handed her a friend's ID. The waitress busted her on the fake ID, confiscated the card and told the girl that her friend would have to pick it up at the police station the next day. I guess it's hard to laugh when you just threw your friend under the bus.

are. I have to shout, "Yes!" and then everyone turns to look at me. I waive and wait for my intro to be read.

I've also been booed when it was announced that I do clean comedy. This was for 500+ people in a retirement home no less. During the show, which went great, I pointed out to them that they were laughing at clean comedy. I think clean comedy has a bad reputation because people don't think it's funny, and I've had clients on occasion take out the word "clean" from my intro because they don't want their group to know that they hired a clean comedian.

I laugh at all these intros, and I can usually overcome them with some humor, or I go into my act and people forget that I'm supposed to be a "working girl." But the thing I can't overcome (aside from a loud crowd) and the thing that really hurts the event is when there's *no introduction*.

When they tell me to just go out and "do my comedy skit," you can bet that it's going to be a little rocky in the beginning.

Of course there are other things that have preceded my comedy show that can make it a challenge.

Getting Laid Off

Not me, the group. I once got to perform for a whole bunch of unhappy people who had recently been told that they were going to be unemployed because the CEO was selling his company. He had announced it a few days before the event, and the client warned me that people weren't happy about it. Really, do you think? You know, comedy can fix a lot of things, but it can't do much about unemployment. I figured I was walking into a room in which everyone was staring at their watches, waiting for me to finish so they could go polish up their resumes.

And the atmosphere was tense. That is, until, about 30 minutes before the show, when the CEO got a call that his sale did not go through. He was pissed off, but the employees were elated. He made this announcement right before I went onstage. I think my intro was something along the lines of "And now here's the comedian," before he stormed out, probably to find another buyer for a company whose employees all would soon be gone. The show went great, but in all honesty, I could've done shadow puppets on the wall and everyone would have been just as happy.

In a similar circumstance, I was booked for a show, and during the client call, they insisted that I not do any of my work jokes, especially my "take the copier" joke. Considering that I'm called "The Work Lady," it might be a little unusual if I didn't at least mention work. I kept asking what the problem was and wondered if they didn't like those jokes. Finally, the client fessed up. They had just laid off a bunch of people, and, you guessed it, those people stole office equipment! How hilarious. My office jokes would have KILLED! Take the copier . . . please! But this was one of those times that I just couldn't say those jokes, and so I wisely let a great comedic opportunity pass.

Off-Color Jokes

Occasionally at these convention gigs, the boss will tell me I can "cut loose" and "be edgy." Telling me to "cut loose" makes me edgy because I'm not sure they understand that I'm going to do a clean show. I really don't have a lot of "cut loose" get down and dirty jokes, and if I did, I still wouldn't do them because it's hard to explain to the client or, if applicable, the agent why I got "blue." But the fact that I don't tell dirty jokes doesn't mean the person introducing me won't. I was performing for a group at a banquet in which the head of the organization started off with, "So a Jew and a plumber walk into a bar . . . ." I kid you not. It was actually a funny joke and had nothing to do with the guy being Jewish. I guess the introducer just wanted to "cut loose" by tossing that in. The joke got a huge laugh, which made me question how my material was going to hit, but my show went fine, too. Afterwards, I headed out to the parking lot and had some attendees come up to tell me how funny I was. All I could think of was, "I need to get to my car before they see the equal rights bumper sticker."

The myriad of things that have preceded me onstage is amazing. Things such as another comedian whose closing bit was humping the bar stool. I got onstage, looked at the stool and said, "I *was* gonna sit on that." I've followed dancing girls, drunken clients, comedians and speeches on healthcare reform. (They kicked off their conference with it and I followed. The client said, "Thank goodness you picked things up!") I've followed memorials to those who have passed away in the organization, millions of awards and a nun who was shaking people down for more money at a fundraiser. (My response: "Hey, Sister Susan just said we are halfway through building the new hospital, and we are $8 million dollars short. How many people think we should not tell that to the construction crew?") I always pay attention to what goes on ahead of me, so I can plan my recovery before I hit the stage!

WISDOM

Pay attention to little things that may be hurting your efforts.
How many times in life do we get a chance to fix something, before it's a problem, yet we don't because we're too distracted with all of the other moving parts? And then, BAM, the one little thing, like a bad introduction, creates an unnecessary headache.

Explain, explain, explain.
I now explain why I ask that they don't clear dishes during my show or read my jokes in my intro, and I've had fewer introduction problems. People who don't do something a lot, like introduce comedians, need to know not just how to do it, but why it's crucial to do it a certain way, and then they get it.

You must set the tone you want.
Whether you're buying a car, meeting a potential date or looking for a job, set your own tone for the interaction, and whomever you're interacting with will be more attentive.

chapter five

We've Got an Idea!

I once did a show for 400 people and they held a "reverse raffle" in which, at the end of a long night, right before I went on, they called out the names of the people who didn't win $1,000. Guess what people do when they don't win something? We whittled that group all the way down to 30 people before I got on. Those 30 had to wait until after my show to see who won the money. Brilliant idea? Not so much.

Nothing good ever comes from those four words when you're talking about a comedian and an event. I've learned that the hard way. "We've got an idea" usually means a few committee members want to pull a fast one on the boss, or perhaps they were just at a retreat where they were challenged to do some "out of the box" thinking, so they're trying it out. Whatever the case, I think some ideas should be buried for all time so that no committee in the rest of history will attempt them again, ever. OK, at least these gems should not be attempted by me. I've struggled on more than one occasion when I tried to comply with a committee's crazy/whacky/brilliant/innovative idea that they want me to attempt.

And I have to take most of the blame. In many cases I was trying to please the committee, but I didn't know what I was doing or I didn't do good enough research to figure it out. And in some cases, I was uncomfortable with the idea, but I didn't want to rock the boat by protesting, so I let the boat sink with me at the mike. Not all of these gigs were bombs, but some of them came close.

Digging Myself in a Hole from the Get-Go

Let's see, I once had a group who told me to go up and interrupt their CEO during his speech and then start in with my comedy. Yes, that's right *interrupt the CEO during his speech*! Maybe that's something a few committee members wanted to do to him, but it's not something that should ever be done, to *anyone*. Luckily, the CEO was in on it, but that's still a really bad idea, because interrupting someone during their speech is rude and makes you look like a jackass. And believe me, it's hard to recover from jackass status even if you're funny. In fact, when you go into your jokes right after interrupting someone, the audience doesn't know that they are jokes, and you look even worse. Recovery is hard.

Now in this instance, the audience didn't hate me. That story is later. I just think that they were too stunned to even laugh. I learned that you can't interrupt the CEO and then start telling jokes about your nieces and nephews because the whole audience is still at, "What the heck did she just do?" I stopped a few times to let them know I'm a comedian. That's a sure sign of a bad show, if you have to let them know to laugh. I finally skulked off the stage. I think the committee members were in the back playing "rock, paper, scissors" to see who had to take credit for that idea. On second thought, they probably just blamed it on me.

And speaking of doing dumb things onstage, have you ever heard of something called an "imposter"? That's a comedian who pretends to be another person, like a new employee or a sales person from an affiliate company. The imposter starts out with a speech about the company, and then gradually gets funnier and funnier or, in some cases, crueler and crueler toward the CEO or the company, until the group realizes, "Hey, this can't be a new employee." People who do this imposter thing get a lot of money, because to pull it off, you have to be good. Remember that whole thing about not starting out as a jackass? Well, the comedians who do this kind of gig excel at starting out as a jackass; the difference is they are experts at digging themselves out quickly and getting the audience on their side—pretty much the opposite of what I did during my CEO-interruptus gig.

I once had an offer to do eight shows for one group, but in order to book any of them, I had to be available for all eight shows. The date of the first show, I was already booked somewhere else. I called that agent and told him the situation, but I sincerely said I would still do his show if he wanted me to and skip the eight shows. He was kind enough to talk with the client and get me out of it. I sent the agent his commission on that show anyway, and those eight shows turned into 40.

With that said, I've still been asked to be an imposter, and I've done it. And though I've never really wanted to be an imposter because I want people to have a license to laugh and to know I'm a comedian, the few times I've done it have not always been disasters. The times it worked well were a blast. Let's start with a couple of those.

Three times I've done this imposter thing in front of sales groups, and they were great. Maybe it's something about sales people, because they're usually good laughers anyway and they get jokes quickly. One time I was introduced as a new person from "corporate" to talk about the teambuilding venture that they had been rolling out over the past two years. Everyone in the company was sick of this teambuilding theme, and so the groans were real and loud. Luckily this theme lent itself to some humor and I was able to start off right away making fun of the theme. Plus, for once, I think alcohol was a little booster in my favor. I kicked off with, "You know, when things are going well with a company, that's the time to mess it up with a new teambuilding venture." And then I went from there. About 10 minutes in, everyone was figuring out that I was a comedian, and the place went nuts. Later in the elevator, two attendees told me that one of them had thought I was for real and the other knew I just couldn't be. I felt great.

> I was once the second choice for a group who had a series of four shows. They booked me for the first one because their first choice was unavailable. The client liked me so much they canceled the comic they had booked for the other three and hired me.

I also did the imposter thing twice at another sales conference and it rocked. On the first day, I did it just for the staff of the organization. I was introduced as the sales manager from the hotel, and I was giving their staff a big "welcome to the property" speech. Luckily the company CEO, who was not in on the joke, had a funny last name and a sense of humor. I started thanking him and then commenting on his name, and then commenting on his name again and again, and I went from there. The place was cracking up, though I finally had to fess up that I really was not from the hotel. The next day, I did the same thing, but for the bigger conference, in which I joked about the conference, and it hit great again.

So three successful imposter events and, even though I was nervous and unsure of them, they turned out beautifully. But you know that saying that "it works until it doesn't"? Well, I hit the time where it didn't, and it wasn't pretty. Picture a thousand people at a major company. The event planner started our preconference planning call with the dreaded, "We've got an idea." They wanted to introduce me as a new employee, and then I would start making fun of the company while gradually going into my act.

I still was shaky about it, but I told them that if they wanted me to, then I'd try it. Bad idea! The purpose of this conference was to pump the employees up. And nothing pumps people up more than having an imposter comedian come out and make fun of the company—not! They were proud of their company and their accomplishments, and what was this jackass new employee trying to do by coming out and making fun of it? I bombed big and abandoned my persona about five minutes into the act. But alas, it was too late, the damage was done. The audience was torn between being confused and insulted. It was not pretty. I made the mistake of thinking I could joke around about the company. I'd done that before and it worked. What was happing with this gig? I wrapped up early, to the relief of everyone, and headed out. Have you ever tried to slip out of a convention in which everyone saw you and pretty much didn't like you? I've had to do that walk of shame across the bar gig floor, but this was an entire convention center. I went to my room and held myself hostage in it until I got the sweet relief of my flight out of there. Now when I hear "I've got an idea," I sometimes think, "Let's stifle your idea and just let me do my act."

Sometimes I wonder, "How did all this happen, when all I wanted to do was be a comedian?" Which leads me to . . .

WISDOM

Never just try anything.
Commit to it fully and give it your best effort. Be 100 percent excited about any new venture you take on; otherwise, you won't put in the effort needed to really make it work. I tried some things that I was uncomfortable with, so I didn't put in my best effort by doing research on it; hence, it blew up in my face. Go for new ideas that stretch you . . . but only if you're totally on board with it.

Know what you are good at and focus on finding your match.
Excel at your strong points (which for me are writing and telling jokes) and pass on the stuff that you aren't good at and the stuff that you don't want to be good at.

chapter six

Getting into Comedy

The most common questions people ask me are about how and why I got into comedy. Well, I've always wanted to do it. When I was 10 years old, I announced to my parents that when I turned 16, I was going to buy a motorcycle, drive cross-country from our house in Virginia to Los Angeles and become a comedian. Based on their reactions, I realized my parents weren't exactly on board with my idea. That was probably in part because I wasn't ever really the class clown growing up. I tried to inject humor into things, but you wouldn't think of me as the funny girl.

My Earliest Attempts at Comedy

I mentioned my duties of "joke of the day" at the lunch table in junior high school, and I took a journalism class in eighth grade in which I tried honing my humor. We had to write a fake newspaper, complete with fake articles, so I made mine funny. Unfortunately, I got in trouble when many of the articles were about the teacher, including something about her posing nude for *Playboy*, resulting in the magazine's "worst sales ever," and in another article I used the word "abortion."

The teacher called my parents and I learned a lesson about appropriate humor.

A friend of mine also nominated me during senior year in high school for the "funniest" superlative. I got two votes—hers and mine. I mentioned in Chapter 1 that I was a funny tour guide, too. Twenty years after I left that job, I read a newspaper article about tour-guiding in D.C. One of the jokes I used to do was featured; it was about Francis Perkins, a woman who was head of the Department of Labor for 12 years. The joke (which was told to me by my supervisor) was, "She was in labor longer than any other woman in history!" The newspaper reported that the tour guide who said that joke got fired. Times changed, I guess.

Those starts and stops are about as far as my comedy dream went for a long time. I ended up graduating from college with a degree in communications, but the dream never went away. I remember at my college graduation dinner, looking around at my family and thinking, "Now is not the time to tell my parents that I want to be a comedian." So instead, I headed into the job search and wound up with a lot of fun marketing jobs over the next dozen

My best friend in the comedy business was a guy named Rob Duffett. He was not even in the comedy business full-time. He kept his "day job," but he started out at the open mikes with me and encouraged me tremendously. We wrote together for many years, and my fondest memories are of sitting on his deck in Adirondack chairs coming up with lines that we thought were brilliant. He passed away last year, and I truly miss laughing with him. He was a great inspiration and helped calm me in times of comedy terror. His signature line was, "All is well."

years. But still the itch to tell jokes stayed with me. I think when you're really, really called to do something, you just can't ignore it. You might be able to put it on hold for 20 or 30 years, but eventually you'll wind up doing at least something related to it. And so I found myself still wanting to be funny professionally. I used to look out my office window and wonder, "What do those people walking around wearing jeans in the middle of the day do for a living?"

I also took a comedy class during this time. Our last assignment was to develop a five-minute comedy routine that would be judged by the teacher's wife and his mother. I got a lot of laughs with mine, and several classmates, as well as the teacher and his relatives, told me I should go onstage. I still didn't. But I did try my hand at an open mike. During the 80s boom in comedy clubs, I went up at a local club and crushed with a killer three minutes. The only problem was, I was petrified; I didn't realize that you are blinded by lights and literally can't see the end of the stage, let alone the people in front of you. As I left the club all freaked out, one of the professional comics followed me outside, grabbed my hand and pleaded with me: "You have got to do this! Please, please, please promise me you'll do this again." I wish I could remember his name. I also wish I had taken his advice, but instead I waited another 10 years, when the comedy club boom with all the great club money had passed, before I tried it again. Timing in comedy is everything, but my timing for getting into comedy was lacking.

Taking Chances with the Pros

One day at work, when I lived in Virginia, I heard on the radio that there was a nationwide comedy contest and the winner would appear on "The Tonight Show" with Jay Leno. You had to send in a five-minute tape of material, to be postmarked by the Friday after Thanksgiving. Great! I dusted off the jokes from 10 years earlier, and found that I was a little short on material. No worries, I thought. Thanksgiving is in a couple days. My family is funny. I'll just make notes and write some jokes about them.

The only flaw in my plan was that nothing much happened on Thanksgiving. No burnt dinner, no crazy relatives visiting, nothing. The only thing I scored on was a tape recorder. I didn't have a way to record my jokes, but I knew my dad had one of these high-tech mini tape recorders. (It was the 90s.) I wanted to borrow it, but I didn't want to tell him what it was for because I was embarrassed. Saying that I wanted to be a comedian had not gone over so well 20 years earlier. When I finally got the courage to ask him, he asked why I wanted it. I held my breath and said there was a comedy contest that I wanted to enter. Luckily, my sister-in-law Robin was sitting next to me, and she said, "Oh, you're naturally funny. You'll probably do well." I was so relieved. My dad just shrugged and handed me the recorder, probably thinking "another one of Jan's nutty ideas."

But still no new material. I woke up the next day, the day the tape was supposed to be postmarked, and I was tired. I also didn't have anything to write jokes about, so I figured, "Forget this contest," and I rolled over to go back to sleep. Then a weird thing happened. In my day job I went to trade shows where I got a lot of giveaways from exhibit booths. That year alarm clocks seemed to be popular, and I had a dresser drawer full of them. I had never used them, but right after I rolled over to go back to sleep, all, and I mean all, of the alarm clocks went off. It was really weird. By the time I dug around and got them turned off, I was wide awake. I decided to write some jokes, and somehow, I got my five minutes of material.

I recorded them by walking around my condo reading them into the tape recorder. It didn't even occur to me that everyone else in the contest would be sending in a tape of a *live* show. I made the postmark deadline, and the next week a woman from the local TV station sponsoring the contest called. She said that I was selected as one of about 25 comics who would be performing my "act" at one of three clubs. I was floored. I blurted out, "How many people actually entered in this thing—two?" She said it was more than 100.

One of the first clubs I emceed for was the Thoroughgood Inn Comedy Club in Virginia Beach, Va. One night I tried to be "edgy" by cussing. The owner, Dean Spearhaus, said afterwards, "Jan, you have a good act. I don't think you need to cuss." I respected his opinion and was flattered that he even paid attention to my act. I cut out the profanity.

I was scheduled for the third night of the competitions, but I still didn't realize what I was getting into until that first night. Arch Campbell, a local TV personality, was emceeing each event, and the first night was held at a club in Maryland. I watched on TV as he reported on the 11 o'clock news, saying that professional comedians are vying for a shot at "The Tonight Show." I sat bolt upright in bed. Did he say *professional comedians?* It was the first time I considered that I might be the only one in the contest who had never been onstage. An open mike a decade earlier and a comedy class did not count. I got up and started pacing—and practicing. About the only thing I remembered from my open mike debut was the blinding stage lights, so I practiced my "act" with a light shining in my face. I can't believe I didn't burn my retinas out.

The night of my contest came around, and true to form, I was the only one of the eight comics on the show who had never performed professionally. I was terrified. I had told some friends of mine that I was doing the competition, but I made them swear not to come out. My friend Cheryl didn't listen to me and brought a group anyway. I was upset at first but then glad I had some people in my corner.

We comics got together to decide what order to go in. I didn't want to go first, so I blurted out, "I'll go fourth." All the comics stared at me and the guy organizing it said, "Uh, we draw numbers." I was totally embarrassed. Of course, we draw numbers, otherwise nobody would go first! I ended up with number five. Whew.

The competition started and I popped in and out of the room. I didn't want to stay in too much for fear of psyching myself out by seeing professionals performing, and my mantra that night was "just don't bomb." I got a little bit of confidence when I saw one professional struggle. I didn't think he was that funny, and so I thought, OK, now I've got a baseline. I think I can be funnier than him.

And I was. I had a pretty good set, with some stuff hitting and some stuff not, but I didn't totally bomb, so I was thrilled. After the show, a woman from the audience told me how much she enjoyed my act, and she and my friends encouraged me to continue. And while I didn't win, the next day at work, my friend Evelyn, who knew I'd entered the contest, casually mentioned that she saw my name in the newspaper. WHAT? She thought I knew about it. They had printed an article about the competition, along with my name and one of my jokes, mentioning me as an example of one of the better, "but inconsistent," acts! I doubt many people saw that article though. I called my mom, who then ran over to the newspaper office and bought up all the extra copies.

My First Big Break

Now you'd think I would've quit my job and headed back to the stage the next week and wound up where I am today. Not so. I kept my job in Virginia and waited another year before I finally decided to try another open mike to get this comedy thing out of my system. I remembered the lights, so I once again blinded myself with a table lamp as I practiced my material. I was nervous that night, and got even more nervous when we drew numbers. (I learned my lesson about blurting things out!) I drew number one. Yikes! I was terrified. I did not want to go first, and neither did pretty much every other newbie comic there, except for one guy, to whom I shall be forever grateful. He was so nervous that he wanted to be first to get it over with, so he traded with me for fourth. I never saw him at an open mike again . . . probably because he went first.

I got onstage with my five minutes of material, mostly from the competition the year before, and I killed! Halfway through my set, I forgot the last two minutes of material. A little voice in my head said, "They're laughing, get off the stage now!" So I did.

As I sat at the table watching the other acts, I had a see-saw going on in my head. Part of me thinking, "That was fun. I want to do it again," and the other part was thinking, "You are not a comedian. Let it go." Then I got a tap on the shoulder. It was the emcee. He was one of the pros, which meant he was making money at this comedy thing, and he said words I will always remember: "Pat caught your act. She wants you to call her." I said, "Who's Pat?" He said, "She books this club and she wants to give you some emcee work."

Sometimes life changes and you don't notice, and sometimes it shifts so suddenly that you can actually feel it. I experienced the latter that night when, I swear, I felt my entire world change. I left that club feeling like I was flying and absolutely knowing that this is what I was going to do. No more second-guessing, no more putting it off, no more marketing job. OK, I actually stayed in the marketing career for another couple of years while I built my comedy career, but I now had a goal and a new life plan.

Now I'm a Paid Comedian!

My first booking through Pat was to emcee for Kevin Nealon from "Saturday Night Live" at the Comedy Café in D.C., but his date got moved, so I was put with a very funny comic magician, The Amazing Jonathan. He now has a room in Vegas, and I would highly recommend you see his show if you're there. But this first booking was six weeks after my first open mike. I had five minutes of what I thought was solid material, and I invited family and friends to come out to my first show on a Friday night. I was psyched. And then that night, the unexpected happened. Right before the show began, Pat told me, "Our feature act didn't show up. You need to stretch until I find a replacement." My five minutes had to turn into 25 minutes fast. If I thought I was nervous about doing five minutes at an open mike, this was the kind of nervous that will make you wet your pants! I had to stretch my newly written act in an A-room (meaning a top club) my first time on a professional show, with my family and friends in the audience.

> The first time I was asked for an autograph was weird. I thought, "I'm just a marketing person." It took a while to shed my marketing persona and really "feel" like a comedian.

I've gone onstage with my knees shaking only a couple times in my career, and this was one of them. Luckily it was a hot crowd and I made fun of everything and everyone that I could. About 22 minutes in, I was doing well but still scared to death. I kept staring at the light hoping it would come on, signaling me to wrap up. It even crossed my mind, "I'm not a real comedian. I have a marketing job. I can put this mike down and walk off stage right now. I may never work again as a comedian, but so what?" I was contemplating just that when the light flashed. The backup feature act had arrived and I was saved. I don't remember what I said about him, but I'm pretty sure it was an awful introduction, something like, "Here's some guy whose going to make you laugh," or "Thank God, the comic is here and I can leave," because he got onstage and said, "Wow, I've never been introduced like *that* before."

He did great though, and then The Amazing Jonathan went up and he was, well, amazing—until his last trick. He said he left it in his car, and could the emcee come up and do another five minutes while he went to get it. He wasn't kidding. I stood there looking stunned. I had used up every bit of my five minutes of material and then some, and there was nothing else to make fun of in the entire room. I must have looked really panicked because the feature act came to my rescue. He tapped me on the shoulder and said, "Do you want me to do it?" I couldn't get the word "yes" out fast enough. He saved me by doing another great five minutes; I probably wouldn't be here today if I had to go back on that stage. The rest of the weekend went off without a hitch. It was eye-opening in many ways. Things that I didn't realize, like comedians use a lot of the same audience lines in each show, gave me a great education in comedy that I wasn't getting at the open mikes.

After that gig, I started getting work in the one-nighter arena, and I went from being top dog at the open mikes to being chewed up and spit out on the bar room stages. I learned very, very fast that open mike comics were one thing, and paid working comics were a different animal.

Eventually, after a couple years and many gigs, I had made all the plans to jump from the day job into comedy full time, but the last detail was telling my parents. That Father's Day, my brother and I were talking in his kitchen about leaving my day job, when my dad walked in. He said, "You're not quitting your job until you have another one, are you?" I took a deep breath and said, "Comedy is going to be my job." To my dad's credit, he told me that maybe I should pursue what I wanted to do. He had always wanted to open his own law practice, and never did, so I think he understood a thing or two about following your dreams.

My parents were my biggest supporters, and they would actually grill chicken and load me up with other food for my traveling cooler so I could save money on the road. They were also my first visitors when I moved to Los Angeles. And before she passed away, my mom told me how proud they were of me. At her funeral, several of her friends said things like, "Oh, you're the comedian? Your mom always told us what a tough job that was and how well you were doing with it." Of course, I invited my parents only to the good clubs, like my home club, the D.C. Improv. The managers always made me look good by comping my parents' tickets and giving them free drinks. I did not bring my parents to the bar gigs! And before the shows, I prepared my dad by saying, "These are jokes about the family. Don't get mad; they are just jokes!" They also loved hearing me on the radio interviews, which made me look even more important in their eyes.

Hitting the Road

My comic friends were making a good living doing one-nighters. These were easier gigs to get than clubs, and the pay was better even though they were usually in bars. Many times the big clubs in the big cities didn't pay as much or provide hotel accommodations for the emcee or feature acts because they had a ton of local acts; they didn't need outsiders. But I knew I wanted to work good clubs because I figured I'd be around great acts. So I drew up a list of the biggest and best comedy clubs in the biggest cities in the country, and then I drew up a list of every single person I knew—family, friends, friends of family, family of friends. I then cross-referenced these two lists and started making phone calls. Ta-da! That was my first marketing plan! I had a couch to sleep on and a good club to work; pretty basic, but it was effective.

Aside from my marketing plan, I brought my work ethic from my marketing career into my comedy career. I had two rules. I vowed to never walk offstage in the middle of a hard gig, but rather to "do my time." And I vowed to never cancel a gig for better money or anything else, unless it was a career move. To date, I've never quit a gig and I've only canceled once, when I won an HBO contest. I was already booked to emcee the weekend that I was to fly to Los Angeles, so I called the booker and explained. I figured I'd never work his club again, but, thankfully, he was thrilled for me. I sent him a tee-shirt from Comic Relief and all was well.

So that's the how and the why of my comedy career beginning. I got into comedy because I wanted to, and these steps, along with many other things I mention in this book, are how I did it. When people ask me how they can do it, I'm happy to tell them, but I preface it with, "I'll tell you how to be a comedian, but you're not going to do it." I know most people won't tolerate some of this craziness. But doing comedy has made for an interesting life for me!

WISDOM

Don't look at what you're leaving. Look at what you're going to.
I had many starts and stops in comedy because I was looking at what I was leaving—day job, financial security, known headaches—instead of looking at what I could eventually get to—a fun career in a profession that I loved.

Stay at the bottom as long as you can.
You can learn a lot, make mistakes and hone your skills when you're at the bottom of the ladder, in my case, as an emcee. A comedian, Lord Carrett, gave me sage advice when he said, "Don't worry about being stuck as an emcee." He said if you get really good at what you do in the "no pressure spot," you won't stay at the bottom. You'll move up. But if you move up too fast, when you're not ready, then you may struggle and get stuck in the middle instead of moving to the top.

Put together some kind of game plan.
My first marketing plan was simple but effective, and I developed some core rules for booking and canceling a gig. These guidelines helped when I had to make a decision about something that was new to me.

Stop asking for permission.
I didn't get into comedy for a long time because I didn't think of myself as a comedian. It was like I needed someone to tell me it was okay to try it. That mindset wasted a lot of time.

chapter seven

Drunks I Have Known

One-nighters were sometimes a source of stress for me and so a lot of times I dreaded doing them. Some of them went great, but it's the ones where I went down in flames that I remember most and that I flash back to each time I got booked in one. And when you go into something with that mental attitude, it's hard to win. I knew I had to quit doing them before I felt so bad about my act that I quit the business altogether. But they were a source of great material because of the mix of alcohol and people.

"Thinkin' Jokes"

I was doing a one-nighter in a small eastern town the Saturday night before Easter Sunday. This particular gig did not come with a hotel. Read the chapter on hotels (Travel Trials) to find out why I wasn't disappointed. It was only four hours from my house, so I figured I could finish by 10 p.m. and head on home. I was coming from another one-nighter the previous night, so I got to this gig around noon. When I walked into the bar, I noticed that much of my audience was already drinking. Great, another one of these, I thought. I had to hang out somewhere for eight hours, so I introduced myself to the owner and asked where the library was. I love libraries, especially while on the road, because they are quiet and comfortable. Well, you'd have thought I'd asked for a ride to the moon. Everyone at the bar looked at me and started laughing. Yes, laughing. The owner explained, "We've had comics come in and ask where the mall is or where the grocery store is, but *never* the library!" I'm guessing to these people, the library was something you were forced to visit while in school, but why on earth would you go there on your own? Well, I persisted and it took three guys to figure out the directions to the library. Great.

I got there and it was closed. A Saturday. School's out. No one in the town is forced to go to the library. This poor library didn't have a chance. So I ended up at the mall, but after a couple hours of hanging out with kids who really should've been at a library, I decided I'd go back to the bar and read my book. I figured I better not tell 'em that I had spent money on a book though, because that is money that could have gone for a beer. When I arrived, the same crew plus a few others were at the bar. One guy turned around and yelled, "Did ya find the library?" and everyone laughed like it was some inside joke about learning. I told them it was closed and asked for a Coke. The owner looked confused and blurted out, "You don't drink either?" Well, I could have countered with, "It's Saturday afternoon. I have a show tonight for *your* audience and then a four-hour drive." But that was too logical, so instead I said, "Ya know, normally I do, but tomorrow being Easter, I'm holding back so I can do my religious material tonight." You could have heard a pin drop and for a minute they were terrified. Then I said that I was joking. That was the first joke of mine that they didn't get, but unfortunately it wasn't the last. The night was awful and I probably should have started drinking with them that afternoon. If I drank too much to drive, I could have always stumbled over to the library and broken in. No one would've ever noticed.

Of course, not laughing at my joke when I first meet them isn't the only thing a bar owner can do to alert me that the crowd is gonna be tough. One bar owner, upon seeing me and realizing that I didn't look like I'd fit in with his patrons, blurted out, "You ain't got any of them 'thinkin' jokes,' do ya?" He was apparently afraid that I was going to educate his crowd or that they would go "a-thinkin,"and perhaps realize that they shouldn't be sitting in a bar every night. He was right. They did not like my little "thinkin jokes." That, too, was a long night. And there was also the one-nighter in which the people were so drunk that, after the show, one really nice woman came up and apologized for her whole town. She said she had lived there her whole life and that was the first time she was embarrassed because of them. How sweet.

> *I've only been heckled a few times, but I did figure out how to deal with someone yelling out stuff. I don't respond to him but rather direct my comments to his girlfriend or wife. The woman he's with will usually get him to shut up.*

Dressed-Up Drunks

Once I got into the convention market, I was pretty much done with the one-nighters, thankfully. But that didn't mean I was done with drunk people. There were still drunk people and one of them might be the CEO, so I had to be more careful. At one event, I started out on a stage, but I didn't wind up there. There were about 500 people at this show, and I got one of those awful introductions where the audience is drunk and loud and the introducer is quiet and inhibited, plus the sound system was through the ballroom speakers in the ceiling— speakers I'm sure they borrowed from the exhibit hall.

When I took the stage, besides the meeting planner and the guy who introduced me, pretty much no one knew I was up there. About 10 minutes into my set, I had a choice: stand on the stage for another 35 minutes and be ignored, or try to get their attention. I really had nothing to lose, so I jumped off the stage, drug a chair to the middle of the room and stood on that. At least I was in the mix and people had to acknowledge this nutty woman. I was able to almost force people to listen and I even got a couple laughs. I usually don't move around much onstage, but standing on a chair will really make you conscious of your feet. There was still one table of really drunk people who wouldn't shut up, and the meeting planner told me later that it included the president of her association, so she couldn't do anything. I hope they elected a new one.

When it comes to drunk people, I've experienced more than just standing on a chair. Have you ever seen someone chug wine from a bottle? And I don't mean someone who was in college at the time or on a reality TV show competing to win 20 bucks. I mean someone who is sitting next to their boss at a company event. Actually the boss was pretty drunk, too, as was everyone in the company. I've never been pregnant, but I'm pretty sure I now know how it feels to go to a party and be the only one who can't drink. This was a holiday party, and these events seem to have their own special brand of drunkenness, with people taking their anger and frustration out on the company by doing damage at the bar.

The biggest compliment I got at this event was, "You were so funny that I waited to leave to go pee until you were done." At least I was getting laughs from these drunks. This was my last show of the year and it was for a law firm, whose employees were probably creating enough lawsuits to keep themselves busy for the next year just at this party alone. It was insane drinking and laughing (with each other and me) and talking and commenting after each one of my jokes. I eventually broke down and pleaded, "You guys, I have 20 more minutes left before the end of my shows for the year. Please hang in there. Right now, I want this year to be over more than you do!" In response, one guy answered a cell phone call very loudly. Let's hope it was from his wife and not a client. Events like these are probably the reason open bars at holiday parties have gone the way of the dinosaur.

One of my worst drunken audience memories involves a booking to emcee an event for an association group. As always, I tried to have a conference call with the client. I say tried because it took forever to get one set up. When we finally did talk, about five minutes into the call with the boss and her assistant, I noticed that the assistant was the only one answering questions, and she didn't have very many answers. I asked about the boss and the assistant told me, "She is on another conference call right now." The woman took another call during our call and her assistant acknowledged that she herself had been with the company only two weeks. I probably knew more about the group than she did because I had read the website!

The only direction I got was that since I was emceeing the show, I was not supposed to do any jokes, and that I must not deviate from the script they gave me. I countered with, "But I'm a comedian." I mean, why hire a comedian when you just want someone to read from a script? I promised them I'd keep it on time and on track, even if I deviated a little from the script to point out some funny things. But no, we will have no jokes from a comedian.

Fast forward to the event. There's a reason I put this story under "drunk stories" because that's how this group was—loud and inebriated. If you combined all the drunks at my one-nighters, comedy clubs and convention shows, there would still be more alcohol at this one event.

It was an awards banquet, and the attendees showed up drunk and talked loudly through everything. I don't know if they thought that the presence of someone outside their group to emcee the event might make a difference, but it didn't work. There was no way I could talk over them, though that didn't stop me from trying. And at first I did get them to be quiet . . . for about 30 seconds. I quickly introduced their president, and they immediately began talking and laughing and ignoring him. It never stopped the whole night, oh, except for when someone at a table won an award. I'm not sure how people heard it; I think they were watching the IMAG screens to see their award category and winner name come up. But when someone won, the whole table screamed and cheered and toasted and drank more . . . then went back to talking loudly. It was the weirdest awards event I've ever witnessed. Honoring people by talking through their acceptance speeches? The boss told me that this is how it always was.

> *My sister Debbie has her own business, and whenever she deals with a tough client, she donates a portion of her commission to her favorite charity. That way the icky client's money has done some good for someone.*

Halfway through this disaster, we took a break from giving out awards because, I guess, people really had to use the bathroom. When the break was over, they were about to send me back up when I realized that the sound guy was gone. Ten minutes later I tracked him down in a room far away eating dinner. I got him back, and we started round two of talking and ignoring the awards until we drug this ceremony all the way to the finish line. As I was about to wrap up, the boss turned to me and said, "Hey, we're a little early, do you want to go up and do some comedy?" Hmm, 9:50 p.m. and everyone has been drinking and talking and ignoring me for three hours. I'd rather perform at a one-nighter on free beer night. No thanks.

Floating Drunk People

OK, I've talked about drunk people on land, but what about drunk people on water? I've performed on several boat cruises, and at one particular holiday party the people were drunk, getting drunk or thinking of getting drunk. They sent me up the same time they announced that the buffet was open, so everyone stampeded to it. Those sitting on the other side of the line couldn't see me, and those in line could but they were busy eyeing the roast beef. I asked the client how long to perform, and she said that once we passed a certain monument, I should stop because everyone will want to take pictures and I would be in the way. I think I was in the way from the get-go, and that that monument did not come up fast enough! The problem with cruising, though, is that once I finished, I was still stuck on the boat for another 90 minutes. Short of swimming to shore—something that I briefly contemplated—I was still floating with them. I found a small corner upstairs where I could gaze out the window, and that's how I ended my night.

But you know, drunk people aren't all bad. In fact, many of them still laugh, and if I'm not having a great show, it's not like they'll remember the show or my name the next day anyway. It's the jerks that really get to me as we'll see in the next chapter.

WISDOM

Find a way to amuse yourself.
Whether it's standing on a chair in the middle of the room or making Easter jokes to someone who doesn't "get it," I always try to find a way to make a tough situation fun for me. At least I'll have a good story and a chuckle later.

Realize when it's not you.
This really does take the pressure off. When you've done what you can, but there's no helping the situation, it's much easier to go with the flow and not let the circumstances get to you!

chapter eight

Jerks I Have Known

That title pretty much sums it up. There are clients, comedians and others who just suck the life out of me. The shows go great, but these people still take the joy out of performing. Thankfully, I've had few of these, but some of the ones I've dealt with have really stuck out.

Looking a Gift Horse in the Mouth

Some people just don't know when they have a bargain. I emceed an all-day event for a big group at their company achievement awards. These lucky, overworked people were winning trips to Cancun and France and, apparently, the moon, and they wanted some humor between speeches to keep the people who weren't winning—you know, the ones who didn't work so hard—engaged and happy. The gig paid peanuts, but I did it because I'd never done a full-day corporate emcee event before, so I wanted to try my hand at it. I figured if it didn't go well, no worries. I knew I could at least give them their money's worth, and then I'd know to stay away from corporate emceeing. My plan was to write material on the fly as the event went along. This strategy can be dicey because creativity is a hard thing to turn on and off, but I wanted to give it a shot.

I met with the big boss before the event, and he told me to make fun of any and all of the management staff who were giving out the awards so they could show their staff that they had a sense of humor and could take a joke. His words were, "No topic is off limits." Perfect!

I found out something about myself that day. I am *really* good at corporate emceeing. I was able to roast the management staff like a pro and really rock the room for eight hours and more than 300 awards! I started out by saying, "Welcome to XHZ awards. We have 700 people here and 332 awards. So to the other 368 of you: Enjoy the free coffee." I had people running over to me between awards, feeding me inside information about management and the company. The room was in stitches every time I took the stage, and people were totally engaged in the whole day. *I am a genius . . .* or so I thought.

After the event, where I had given this company a really, really great show for really, really cheap, I thanked the boss for having me. The only thing he said was, "You shouldn't have made fun of 'Ed,' about his height. We don't do short jokes." Really? "Ed" was a manager, who was supposed to be fair game, and I didn't come up with the height thing anyway. One of his staff told me that they goof about his height all the time to his face. Plus, what I said wasn't all that bad: "Thanks for the

Mark Ridley, one of the nicest people in the business and the owner of the Comedy Castle in Detroit, complimented me once by saying that he appreciated my professionalism. I don't drink up the bar. I don't go over my time. And I do what I say I'm going to do.

speech, Ed, but coming from you, we thought it would've been a little bit shorter."

This jerk honed in on this one line in eight hours of almost continuous laughter. I was upset with him, but I was so pumped about how well I'd done that I just let it slide. Maybe because I gave this guy a break on my fee, he didn't appreciate all my efforts.

The Discount Dilemma

I rarely discount my show, but I will if it makes sense, like if I'm already in the area or I'm trying something new, like emceeing. Then I try to accommodate people's budgets within reason. But just about every time I do it, my generosity ends up biting me in the butt. I've learned that some people who get a deal continue to want more of a deal. They'd have me washing their car if they could get it in the contract! And if they don't heap on the extras, sometimes they still turn out to be a royal pain to work with. I once agreed to do a cheapo event for a group because it was scheduled for my lightest month of the year and I was doing it as a favor to a relative, only to have the client change the event to my busiest month. I still tried to accommodate them, but that should have been a huge red flag.

After the date switch, a tsunami of changes, requests and brilliant ideas started flooding in. He had a few bullet points that he'd like me to make during my humor keynote. No big deal. I could do that. Then the phone chats with him and his committee got worse. On one call, he said, "Please don't do any jokes." I reminded him that I'm a comedian and it is a *humor* keynote, and, well, I would like to do some humor. I'm not sure if I got the OK on it, but no one objected. Then another person said that I should know that some of the staff was being laid off, so maybe I should address that and then she went into a rambling speech with ideas about how to do that. I asked her to repeat it because I just didn't follow it, and she started, got lost and finally said, "I don't know how to put it into words." I said I can mention work stresses, but that I don't want to focus my humor on layoffs. Thankfully, they all agreed. Whew!

A few days later, I got the convention program, and there was no mention of my humor, only that I was doing some sort of session focused on his bullet points! I finally told the client that he needed to get another speaker. Since it was about two weeks out from the program, this got their attention. So after many, many, emails and phone calls later, I was allowed to do the humor that we had originally contracted for, along with his bullet points, and it went over great!

Getting Past the Stumbling Block(head)s

And then there are the people who try to intentionally hinder your success and end up losing. I once worked at a comedy club with a headliner who wanted to be famous, so he wouldn't let me do the radio shows with him that the club had lined up. I was featuring at the time and I always asked the headliner if I could tag along so that I could get some experience. Most of them were astonished that any comedian would volunteer to get up at 5 a.m. to go into the station and were appreciative of the offer. The more funny people on the show, the better! Not this guy. He was lined up with three or four radio shows, and when I asked him if I could go along, he said, "No, this is MY show." Fine. I slept in while he did his radio thing.

That night, when I got off stage, the club owner ran over to me and excitedly announced that a representative of the biggest radio station in town, the one she'd been courting for months, had seen my act. The station rep was thrilled that I had clean material (unlike the headliner) and asked if I could be on their station in the morning. Yes! When leaving the club that night, the owner said she'd pick me up around 6 a.m. Upon overhearing this, the headliner asked me what was going on and I told him about the biggest station wanting me on their show in the morning. He looked stunned, and before he could say anything else, I simply said, "My show."

Unfortunately, he wasn't the only headliner who gets a spot in the jerk chapter by trying to make it "his show." I once worked with a comic whose sitcom had long since been canceled, and apparently he didn't get the memo that he wasn't a big star. In fact, he thought he was such a big star that he should have most of the stage time, so he canceled the emcee, and I was told I would feature and do emcee duties. Oh, and that my time onstage would be anywhere from two to 45 minutes. That's right, two to 45 minutes. I was to perform until I saw the "light" and then I needed to wrap up. That should've been my first inkling that he was trying to sabotage my set by not letting me plan it.

> Sometimes the people aren't jerks so much as just clueless. I once had a guy call me to change the time of the show; turns out he meant the date. Big difference! I found this out the day before I was scheduled, and I still made it.

The first night, I was 40 minutes into my set, wondering when this guy is going to show up, when I finally got the light. I jumped to my closing bit and then introduced him. Second night, the room manager apologetically said that the headliner didn't like it that I went to my closing bit. He wanted me off immediately, so when I got the light, just get off stage. OK. The next night, about five minutes in, I got a big laugh a second before I got the light, so I introduced the headliner and left. The "star" then took five minutes to make his way to the stage. I guess this was his grand entrance. The manager assured me I'd done what I was supposed to do. I was having great shows, so I didn't care, but I think it was really irritating this headliner. I could tell he had done this before to comics, with different results.

The third night, I get the light after only about five minutes; again I had just gotten a big laugh, so I exited. This was my first time at this club, so I didn't really know the staff. When I walked by the manager, a guy I'd only met two days earlier, he said he had to ask me if I had used the "N" word (derogatory word for African Americans) in my act. I was shocked. "No," I said, "definitely not." He said the headliner, who was black, had told him he thought he heard me say it. Thankfully, the manager told the headliner that he'd

> At the beginning of the recession a few years ago, I had one client freaking out. In her words, "I can't believe I hired a comedian. We can't laugh; it's a recession!" She put a horrible energy around the room, and the show was less than perfect.

only heard my full act once, but it didn't sound like my style. I asked which joke, and he said that the headliner didn't tell him a particular joke. I was having fantastic shows, even with the little bit of time I was allowed, and this headliner hated it, so he was trying to undermine me with the manager. I was furious and spent the rest of the week hanging out in the office watching TV. I refused to even interact with this jerk.

A year later, I showed up at another club, and guess who's headlining? Yep. He looked at me and said, "Have I met you before?" I said, "Yeah, (insert city)." That was another long week in which I spent most of my time off stage watching TV again. (And no, his sitcom wasn't even fresh enough to be in reruns.) But this time I made my few minutes onstage *really* count. I crammed in so many jokes that the audience was going nuts and it took this guy a few minutes to get them into his act. I have since had other offers to work with this jerk, and I always decline, telling the club owners my story. In fact, I told it to several comedians, one of whom was this guy's best friend before the sitcom, and he agreed with me on the jerk status!

Sometimes it's the comic who wants to be the headliner who is the jerk. There was a guy featuring for me once, who, upon meeting me announced, "I want your job." Great way to introduce yourself, huh? He didn't like being the feature act, so his way of "getting my job" was to try to make me look bad by working the audience into a frenzy; his act was a mix of high energy and dirty humor, pretty much everything I am not. I guess he figured that if I couldn't follow him, the club owner would magically see that he's the better act, and we'd switch places.

I once got cancelled from a gig at the last minute because they found a comic who would work for free. I can't beat that price.

Each show, even though he was asked to work clean by the club owner, his material just got filthier and filthier. At the end of the week, he came up to me very frustrated and said, "I've thrown everything I have at them and you're still able to follow me. HOW?" He was perplexed that my cute kids' jokes could follow his vivid descriptions of bodily functions and sex.

I said, "Why don't you just do your own thing and forget about 'getting' me?" When I was featuring in clubs, I hardly ever blew the headliner away, but I still became a headliner myself because I did my thing, had great shows and the club owners saw it. I'm not sure if he ever took my advice, but I have yet to hear him headlining.

And sometimes it's people in the industry who are the jerks. I got on a showcase at a major club run by an owner who had a lot of pull in the industry. If he liked you, you really could become a star. I got the showcase through an agent who was helping me as a favor; he was not my agent, but he put in a good word for me. Nice guy . . . or so I thought. I went onstage and ROCKED. After the showcase, if you wanted, the club owner would give you a review of your act; if he decided to manage you, your career could soar fast. So when the club owner walked into the room, all the comics swarmed him. He ignored them, looked directly at me and pushed his way through the sea of comics, motioning me to follow him. He told me how impressed he was and that he wanted to meet with me in his office that week. Cool! I had my first big industry meeting. Well, as it happens in entertainment, things don't often work out so smoothly. I got to his office a few days later, and he proceeded to tell me that the agent who had recommended me to him called to tell him that

Watch out for the "stealth jerks." I performed at a convention in which the day before the event, while I was meeting with the client, the big boss came down and started changing everything my poor client had worked on, from the agenda (which was already printed) to the decorations. One person leaned over and said, "What X wants is what X gets." He deflated his whole staff and threw them into unnecessary turmoil. These jerks, in my opinion, while they may have a position with the company that is respected, are really causing more problems than they are worth.

he (the agent) was already my agent. What? That was an outright lie. The club owner was pissed though and thought I had lied to him about not being represented. I was confused and assured him that I was agentless, but to no avail. He told me to sort it out and get back to him.

I immediately called the agent to find out what the deal was. He stammered, hemmed and hawed and said the club owner got it wrong, blah, blah, blah. This guy turned out to be the stereotypical bad industry person (at least to me), not interested in me until I did well on a showcase and then he might be interested, so he scared off the rest of the industry. I called the club owner back, but he did not want to get involved until he heard from the agent, which never happened. And the agent never took my call again. In fact, I once called him, and it went to voicemail, so I immediately called back from another number. He picked up, and when he realized it was me, he did his usual stuttering and stammering around. He couldn't get off the phone fast enough. The club owner always remained very polite to me, but that was about it.

Getting Paid

Yes, the touchy subject of payment. I'm an artist, but I also had to become a business woman really fast. Contrary to popular belief, successful comedians don't just sit around all day writing jokes at Starbucks. Aside from being the funny one, you must be the marketing person, the IT geek and the collection service. I've only been cheated on payments a few times, and in four instances I've actually been overpaid. Each time, I mentioned it to the person in charge, and three of the four times, they let me keep the money! This was back when I really needed the money, and it was much appreciated.

The few payment problems I've had were when I worked for people that I knew in my gut I shouldn't have worked for. When I started out, I had one strict rule for booking work: I'd work for anyone with a pulse. That's the kind of rule you have when money is extremely tight and you're new to the business. And since both criteria applied to me, I ended up working for a club owner I'll call CB (for Crazy Booker). CB had lots of work, and many of us comics worked for CB even though CB was known to have issues: sketchy payment issues, messed-up booking issues and all sorts of general bad-things issues. I didn't have any problems with CB (at first) until one night when CB cut the money on me. "Cut the money" is the comic's nicer term for "cheated." I was booked to perform shows Thursday through Saturday, but the Thursday show at CB's club had no audience. (Apparently marketing wasn't a strong suit of CB's.) At the end of the weekend, CB decided to take $39 bucks out of my pay for some kind of punishment even though I wasn't in charge of marketing. I'm supposed to bring the jokes, not the audience. I was emceeing at the time, and $39 bucks was like $39,000 bucks. It was a huge amount!

The six-hour drive home that night was awful and only further depressing because around 2 a.m. a big pink bus drove by me with the word "Dolly" on its side. Dolly Parton was passing me literally and figuratively. I thought to myself, "I bet Dolly's not dealing with people like this!" And then it hit me: my inner voice said, "And you don't have to either!" After a lot of back and forth in my head, I finally decided that I got into this business to have fun, to work for people I respect and to make money. I was doing none of that with CB. So as frightened as I was to do it, I stopped calling CB for work. I figured I'd stay away for one year, and if I was desperate at the end of the year, then I'd swallow my pride and dial his number.

It is an understatement to tell you what a huge move this was. As a new comic who had few connections, I was considered one of the lucky ones because I got approved for work in these clubs. There were comics who were begging to get into those clubs, and there still were other comics who had been cheated by CB but who continued to work for him because they needed the work. But my gut told me that I just couldn't.

And so the year went by, and not working for CB did affect me financially. I actually made more money! I had to look for work elsewhere through expanding my connections, and my bank account grew during that process. And in a weird move, CB actually called me to find out why I wasn't calling for work. I can proudly say that I never burned the bridge by telling CB what to do with that $39. I just said that I was not available for work because I was booked. And I was.

The Jerk at Table Three

There are a lot of jerks out there, and sometimes we all do jerky things unintentionally, but the people in this chapter made an impression because they were jerks intentionally. And, in my opinion, those are the worst kind. When you think of jerks in a comedy club, most people think of hecklers. Luckily I've never been heckled much, so I don't really have a lot of heckler stories. The few times that's happened, the person has been drunk, so check out Chapter 7 for those.

But audience members can be jerks in different ways, like rooting against you from the start. All comedians have to fight stereotypes because audiences have preconceived notions of your humor depending on what they know about you. If you're fat, the audience may expect fat jokes. If you're black, a lot of times the audience expects "Def Jam comedy" jokes, and if you're a woman, for some reason, they sometimes think either you're not funny or you're dirty. On several occasions, people apologized to me by saying things like, "We saw that a woman was on the show and we told each other that this was going to suck, but you were actually great!" And I once walked up behind some people who were looking at the marquee outside the club, and one woman turned to her friends and said, "Yuck, it's a woman comic tonight. I don't think they're funny." I popped up with, "Hey, we're not so bad!" The woman was mortified, and she slunk away into the club. That night I had a killer set, and every time a joke hit, I looked over at her table, giving her the evil eye. I couldn't really see her because of the lights, but she didn't know that. I just bring this up because I hope in the future, when you see comedy, you will keep an open mind, and not judge comics even before they hit the stage. You might get a really great surprise!

WISDOM

You have more power than you think you do.
Regardless of how little money you have or how much "power" you think someone else has, you must realize your value and not settle by working for those people who treat you badly. They need you just as much as you need them. Remember your power, and know when to move on when someone is not behaving nicely towards you. Do it without hesitating!

Pay attention to the stuff you *don't* do.
I think sometimes I've been booked because I'm easy to work with and don't cause any drama. Pay attention to not being a jerk, and make people want to work with you.

Do your own thing.
Spending energy to make me look bad backfired on those jerks. Focus on what you do best, which will allow you to shine. If you're good at what you do, others will see it, and you'll stand out from the crowd.

Don't put what you value into someone else's hands.
I followed the typical comedy career path of trying to find one agent to represent me. It now scares me to think that, had those agents not been jerks at the start, I would have put my valuable career in their hands and been at their mercy. They taught me to rely on myself.

Validate yourself.
Many people make the mistake of wanting others—in my case, agents or audience members—to tell them their own value. (For me it's that I'm funny.) But you can't look to outside sources to tell you what you can and can't do. Knowing what you're capable of is something that has to come from within. I wonder how many fledgling comedians never got past fledgling because they lost a contest or some jerk told them that they weren't funny, and they believed it.

chapter nine

Travel Trials

I love traveling, and when I left my "day job," I was thrilled to be on the road driving instead of sitting behind a desk. I made the most of it by doing some sightseeing along the way and stopping to just hang out in various spots to enjoy my freedom. I remember once standing on some cliffs in Utah on a Monday afternoon thinking, "I can't believe how lucky I am. Look what I get to do!" As I mentioned, my parents made me food for the road. I think my mom was secretly worried that I didn't have enough money for food, and she wasn't too far off the mark. I also became a "professional guest" at many people's homes. I racked up many, many miles on my car and enjoyed just about every minute of it.

I'm Sleeping Where?

I brought some essentials with me when I first started out. I had a cooler that plugged into my car's cigarette lighter to keep food hot or cold, no ice or heat packs needed. I also had an atlas and a phone calling card because there was no Google or Siri back then. And I had a sleeping bag. I did sleep a couple dozen times in my car in rest areas, but the sleeping bag was really for the beds at some of the places that they put comedians up in, dumps from which, we comics joked, the police had "just removed the body." These places made you worry about leaving your luggage in the room while you were at the show.

I braced myself for this change in accommodations from my travels in my "real job" marketing career, but right before I quit the business world, I had one last business trip to San Jose, where I stayed at the Fairmont Hotel. I spent most of that last night luxuriating in a whirlpool tub while sipping on chardonnay. I knew the fall from the Fairmont was going to be rough!

I knew I had to get a better car when I got into the convention market. Going to one of my first shows at a country club near my house, as I approached the guard's booth, I realized my Honda Civic had 200,000+ miles on it and silver duct tape was holding the door together. Someone had broken into it while I was in Vegas and this was my fast fix.

I don't mind budget hotels. They saved me when I had to pay on my own. In fact, a budget hotel would have been welcome when I was starting out in comedy clubs, but what I'm talking about are under-budget hotels and other places that bordered on illegal. I once spent the weekend sleeping in a room in the rafters of the club, with the doors locked from the outside! And then there's the time I had to stay with the club owner in his kid's bedroom while his kid slept on the couch. Weird, weird, weird.

And sometimes they put us up in a "comedy condo," where you lived with the other comics for the week. It was me and mostly 21-year-old guys. Our lifestyles were a bit different and I'm sure they were a little bummed to see someone closer to their mom's age living with them. A waitress was usually tasked with "cleaning" the condo on her day off. You knew it was her day off because sometimes the cleaning job just screamed, "I'd rather be at the beach." Not all the condos were bad, but there were some memorable ones, like the condo in which one of the prior comics had punched a hole in the wall. Lying on my bed, I could see the outside. And one time, I got approved for work in a great club, but I never followed through on a booking because I heard so many rumors about the seedy neighborhood the condo was in.

And we're not talking everyone gets a bed in a condo. One club owner actually had another comic and me sleeping in a one-bedroom condo. I was the feature act, so the headliner got the bedroom, and my "room" was the couch. We realized it wouldn't work out for a number of reasons. He stayed up until 3 a.m. I go to bed right after the show, and the only TV in the place was in the living room, you know, my "bedroom." That's the only time that I've played the "I'm a woman" card. I put my foot down and said I couldn't share a condo like this with a guy. The other comedian played along by saying that his wife would be angry at the

I slept in many rest areas from Virginia to California and I had a routine. I'd stop at the exit before the rest area to brush my teeth. Then drive to the rest area, park in a lighted spot near truckers and immediately put the driver's seat back and pull a sleeping bag over my head. I used my bladder as an alarm clock because it would usually wake me up in a few hours. The night before I moved to Los Angeles, my parents handed me money and asked me to please not sleep in any rest areas as I crossed the country.

arrangements. The club owner relented and got me a hotel room.

The signage in the condos was pretty funny, too. There were warnings like, "Don't bring the waitresses back!" What generally happened was when a comic got "too cozy" with a waitress, the waitress fell in love, the comedian moved on to another city the next week, and then the heartbroken waitress quit. It might make for a good Julia Roberts movie, but it's lousy for running a business.

When I went into the convention market, I expected to experience a better side of the hotel industry, but one of my first convention gigs was at a conference in Las Vegas at a hotel I had never heard of. I thought no big deal; my comedy career had prepared me for no-name hotels. So as I checked into this Vegas no-name hotel, I wondered if these convention gigs might be the same accommodations as the comedy gigs. The clerk was very nice and as he handed me the room keys. For some reason, out of the blue, he blurted, "You are gonna like this hotel; it's just like the Fairmont!" At that moment, I thought, "I'M BACK!"

But there were some weird places in the convention market, too. In fact, it was a little schizophrenic. One booking you're treated like a queen on the concierge level of a five-star hotel, and the next gig, you find yourself sleeping in a retirement community apartment or a college dorm room. Granted, in these places there is no concern about bodies under the beds.

I once was put up in mom-and pop-motel. I have no problem with that except that the "mom" was really, really snoopy. Once at the hotel, I took a nap. Bad idea. I woke up with the bedside phone ringing. I was so tired that I didn't answer it. But it rang and rang, and rang and rang, which made me crankier and crankier. I then refused to answer it on principal, so I unplugged it. Nobody on the planet knew where I was. What's the big deal? Then came the incessant door-knocking. Apparently one person on the planet knew where I was, and since I couldn't unplug the door, I opened it. It was "mom." She said the guy who booked the room, my client, had left a message at the front desk for me to call him when I can. She said she knew I was in the room because my car was outside, so she wanted me to call him *right now*; she just about dialed the phone for me. I almost snapped and told her about the invention of Post-it notes and answering machines, but I was too tired.

Of course, not all these unusual accommodations were courtesy of the client or club; I got to experience one of those pay-by-the-hour motels . . . by choice! I picked up a gig in a resort town so I could afford to attend a friend's wedding, but the problem with resort towns is that there are no empty hotel rooms on holiday weekends. The club didn't offer a hotel, so I was on my own, and the only one I could find was pretty grim. I walked into the hotel office and a skanky guy, the type who I figured was a regular at these kinds of hotels, followed me in. When I told the clerk that I needed the room for the *whole night,* she gave me a strange look and said, "Well, maybe you should see the room first." I guess this was her version of making me sign a waiver before committing. The room was bad. Shag carpet, that probably didn't start out as shag (think something growing), cigarette burns on the tub and a bed that was just a bit too lumpy. Skanky-man turned to me and the clerk and said, "I can't do this," and ran off. I said, "I *have* to do this, I have no choice." I showered with my socks on, slept at the very bottom of my sleeping bag and left at the crack of dawn. The next night, I opted to sleep in a rest area on my drive home; it was cleaner and safer.

I also chose a weird place to live when I first moved to Los Angeles. I wanted to stay in town more, but I didn't want to take a waitressing job, so I needed to keep my expenses way down. Enter the 400-square-foot studio apartment for 400 bucks a month! I figured it was cheap enough to put on a credit card if I had to. Thankfully, I never did. But it was small. It had three places for people to sit, provided one of those people had to go to the bathroom. There was a chair, a futon and a toilet. I lived there for a couple of years, surrounded by college students attending USC, while I built my comedy career from the West Coast. I have since moved on, but that crappy little apartment allowed me to keep working in this business and move on to better-paying gigs.

> *I was once so broke, that when I got to a toll booth, I had no money. I tried selling the guy some stamps, but he didn't need any.*

Planes, Trains and Automobiles

The other element to travel besides the accommodations is, well, the travel. I've had great luck with airlines because my rule is to take the first flight out in the morning; the plane is not coming from somewhere else, and if there is a problem, you still have a shot at making it to your destination. I only had one weird instance getting to a flight when I was on a cruise ship. I was flying out the morning after the show from this tiny Caribbean town, but before I could leave the ship, two very serious, frightening customs agents sat me down and grilled me about my flight. Like I was going to defect to their country instead of go home! And even if I did, they could probably track me down on the island within the hour. Still, I was duly intimidated and worried I'd give them the wrong answers about my birthdate and address.

So air travel is good to me, but I've had some dicey road trips when I was driving 50,000+ miles a year to comedy clubs. My advice to new comics: Get a good car! Mine broke down all over the country, and it had an oil leak that puzzled mechanics and drained my bank account. Every thousand miles I had to put a quart of oil in it, which isn't so bad except in a *white-out blizzard*. I was going from a one-nighter in North Dakota and trying to make a club in South Dakota during January. Brilliant routing! The white-out hit, and visibility was zero. I kept on chugging toward South Dakota until I called the booker and he said "This is bad, head east." so I did, stopping on some very perilous roads to put oil in my car. I would've worried more about being hit by another car, but nobody else was dumb enough to be out in that weather. And if I did get lost in the snow, I figured rescuers could just follow the oil slick to my car.

But do you know what's worse than a white-out? Fog! You can't clear fog off with your windshield wipers when

Upon arriving on a remote Caribbean island to catch a cruise ship the next day where I would perform, I waited for more than an hour for a car service that was supposed to pick me up to take me to the hotel. No one showed, so eventually a kind taxi driver came over, and when I told him my problem, he said in very broken English he thought he knew where the cruise entertainers stayed. Having no other options, I got in his cab for a harrowing 30-minute ride through small villages and dirt streets. I was either going to be murdered or get to a hotel. I was shocked when I arrived at a very posh resort.

you're driving down a mountain freeway in Vermont at 2 a.m. Thankfully, I wasn't in my oil-guzzling car, but I still had to stop in the middle of the road and get out on a treacherous mountain highway. There was a steep drop-off on my right, and somewhere to my left was the yellow line; the only way to find it was to get out of my car and kneel down close to the road to find the line. This was pre-MapQuest, and the agent had told me the gig was only two hours from the airport; I realized it was more like six hours. I was tired from being on the road for several weeks, and I just wanted to catch my flight home that morning. I did not realize mountains and fog go together.

The fog was so bad that I got lost and ended up in Massachusetts. My flight was out of Albany, New York, and I finally found my way near Albany, but I was completely turned around and the fog was covering up all the signs. By then it was about an hour before my flight, and I was tired. I pulled over and said, "God, I have no idea where I am. Help!" Just then, out of the fog, like in some mystery movie, a cop car pulled someone over. That driver's misfortune saved me as I pulled up next to the cop and got directions. He looked at me funny at first until I explained that my eyes were red from crying, not drinking.

Back to my oil-gulping car, it did finally die for the last time, appropriately, on the road. It had conked out on me quite a bit on one trip from Virginia to Ohio and St. Louis, and every time I shut it off, it took a while to crank back up. My poor car was as tired of road gigs as I was. Whenever I had to stop for gas, I would position it so it would be easy to push to a parking space if it didn't start. If I let it sit for about an hour, it usually would go.

During one of these breakdowns, I found myself on the highway holding jumper cables with a pleading look on my face. A young guy stopped and tried to jump it to no avail, and as he left, he said, "Please tell people that we young people aren't so bad." After he left, a family pulled up in a car that looked worse than mine. The mom jumped out and asked if I was OK; that was very sweet, and I've thought about what a nice role model she was for her kids. The parents looked like they didn't have 10 cents between them, yet here they were trying to help a total stranger in need.

I got the car towed and fixed and back on the road . . . as far as a North Carolina dealership. They have you when your car is towed in! After checking out the car, the woman dealer said in her sweetest southern accent, "Honey, your engine is just plain wore out." She handed me back the keys, and as I cranked it up, thick, black smoke poured out of the engine. I was staying with some relatives that night, so I called them and told them the route I was taking to their house. I said, "If I'm not there in 30 minutes, come looking for me." I made it, but the car totally quit in front of their house, plummeting their property values, I'm sure. I was really upset, but all I could do was kick the tires and call a charity to donate it.

I returned home from that trip in a rental car, and it was one of those stressful days when I thought I don't want to have one drink because I would never stop. No car, not much work booked and the only way to get to any work was with a car. I called my sister to drown my sorrows, and she said to me the words that my mom always said, "It'll work out." And it did. The next day, three bookers called me for work; they never call the comics! I soon got another car and was back in business. The charity called me a few months later to say they got a lot of money for my old car at auction. I told them I didn't want to know what they got. I'm guessing if I ever wanted to find out where that car ended up, I could just follow the oil trail!

Comedians are hard on cars, and so with my next car, while I had a better experience, I still had a few troubles, most notably while I was moving cross-country to Los Angeles. I chose a move date based on the fact that a club in California had booked me; I had lived in California for a few months earlier that year to see if I liked it. I did, so when I got booked, I figured I might as well just move.

I started my trek across the country doing a little sightseeing on the side. On Monday, while I was eating an apple at a rest area in Wyoming, I called the club to find out what time the show started on Thursday, and I heard the recording say I would be appearing starting *Wednesday*! Oops. I jumped in my car and raced toward California. About 1 a.m., I pulled into a gas station, and thick black smoke exploded from beneath my car—not the overheating kind of smoke but a different, more expensive-looking smoke. I was all alone and pretty scared, and as I walked into the gas station, a young guy walked by me and commented, "Wow, your car is smokin'!" I went into the bathroom, looked in the mirror, and thought, "I can't fall apart. I have to figure this out." I walked back outside and the same young man walked by me and said, "Your car is still smoking!" Don't ever say that to someone whose car is smoking.

I asked him if he knew anything about cars and he just walked away. Some other nice local guy called his mechanic friend, but 1 a.m. not really being business hours, he didn't have any luck. I got back in the car, closed my eyes and cranked it up. It started! I figured I'd find a motel and deal with it in the morning, though the drive got even dicier when I saw highway signs warning people not to pick up hitchhikers because of the nearby prison. My mantra became, "Don't break down. Don't break down. Don't break down."

After a few hours of restless sleep I cranked up my car in the morning and it seemed fine. I drove it until I saw a guy who looked like a mechanic standing outside a repair shop. He was nice enough to take a quick look at it, but he couldn't find anything wrong. When I told him I was heading to California, his sage advice was, "Lady, keep on driving." (I've often thought that should be the title of this book.) So that is what I did.

I made it to the club 45 minutes before my show. Afterwards, I was talking to the bartender and I told him I had all my worldly belongings in my car, but I was just too tired to unload. He recalled his own story about driving across the country with all his stuff and being so exhausted when he got here, he left it in his car overnight . . . and it was all stolen. I spent the rest of the night loading all my stuff into the comedy condo.

I had that car for 10 years, and the weird smoking thing happened two other times. I took it to repair shops, but it was as mysterious as the oil leak in my previous car. Oh well.

And, no, I didn't go into the convention market just to stay in good hotels and avoid driving 50,000 miles a year. I made the leap for several reasons, and the way I did it was not really straightforward . . .

WISDOM

Practice living the way you intend to live.
When I was leaving my marketing job, I knew I'd have less money in the beginning, so I started living that way. I don't mean I infested my house with roaches and hookers to get used to gross hotels, but I did pinch pennies and I paid attention to how I felt when I was put up in rough places to make sure I could handle it on a full-time basis. Jumping into something new that drastically changes your lifestyle without testing it is setting yourself up for failure.

Spend the money to get the tools you need.
I could've saved myself a lot of headaches if I had done some research and bought a car suitable for driving 50,000+ miles a year. Don't cut corners on the wrong things no matter what the cost.

There are good people in the world.
Not everyone is a jerk. In my travels, I've encountered some nice people willing to help a woman on the road alone.

chapter ten

Crossing Over . . . from Comedy Clubs to Chicken Dinners

My entrance into the convention comedy market from comedy clubs happened a bit by accident, and like my arrival into comedy in general, I had several starts and stops. As I've mentioned, I knew about the convention market because I had booked entertainment for conferences when I had my marketing job. After a few years as a comedian, I started seriously thinking about getting into convention work. It was a better fit for my act, plus I was pushing 40, so I was kind of aging-out of handling comedy condos and bad hotels. There's a certain point in your life when living with strangers in a condo decorated in early American "college apartment" just isn't appealing anymore. Plus the constant driving and being gone from home for weeks or months at a time was getting to me. I loved being on the road and working the comedy clubs because it was so different from sitting at a desk, but putting 50,000+ miles each year on my car and being gone six days a week, 45 weeks or more a year would make even a travel writer scream, "Uncle!" I once drove across the country three times in one year!

Getting Lemonade from Lemons

Not to get too metaphysical on you, but I think when you put things out in the universe, they really do happen. And I had been putting "I want to work in the convention arena" out there a lot, but I knew I wasn't ready yet, so the universe still had me auditioning to get club work. At these auditions, sometimes called showcases, the protocol is that the emcee goes out and does 10 minutes to warm up the crowd, then the showcasing comics go out and do a hot 10 minutes each to show the club owner how great they are. If all goes well, you get booked.

At one particular showcase, things got a little weird. The feature and the headliner were in the green room fighting over who stole whose material. Apparently they both realized the night before that they had similar jokes, so accusations were flying and fists were about to. The bit they were arguing about was actually a pretty stock bit, so I think they both

One of the great times that I pulled off a risky joke was when I was performing for an Iowa company at their holiday party, and morale was low, low, low because they weren't getting raises. And by the looks of it, they were trying to drink their raises that night at the open bar. I started my show off slow and had some ho-hum reactions. I finally looked around the room and said, "Ya know, I understand you're having a pretty warm winter here in Iowa. In fact, the only thing around here that's frozen is SALARIES." I thought the roof was going to come off the place!

stole it from someone else! The emcee was onstage, and I stood near the stage to get out of range of the angry comics. I thought the emcee would do his usual 10 minutes to settle the crowd, but instead he did three hack (pretty common) car jokes and brought me out to a cold crowd. I was the victim of one of the oldest tricks in comedy: Get the showcaser to warm up the crowd, so the emcee has a great show and gets moved up to the feature position for future bookings. After my not-so-great showcase, the club owner was empathetic about what had happened, but she could only offer me emcee work at one of the other clubs. She said she'd have someone take a look at me and see if they could move me to the feature slot.

Rats! Emcee work paid around $25 a show. I needed the feature money, but there was a lot of work with these clubs if I got in,

I never bring religion into the mix, but it is amazing how many business groups do. I performed at a Christmas party once, back when we could call it a Christmas party, held in a church basement. It was a chicken dinner complete with lemonade and iced tea. No bar, which might not be bad except that the employees were truck drivers. Having driven on the road for years, and stopped at many a truck stop, I know truck drivers like beer. At the beginning of the event, we all held hands in a circle for a long prayer, during which someone's cell phone went off. So a bit later onstage, I opened with, "Hey, during the prayer, someone's cell phone went off. I hope you answered it because it might have been Jesus calling . . . to find out where the beer is!" The place went nuts. They loved it and, more importantly, I got an instant connection with them.

so I figured I'd do one week as an emcee and hope to move up. Fast forward to the week in their club. I got lost on the way there and arrived very late. It's one of the few times that I walked in after the start time of the show, and I had barely enough time to change my shirt and no time to chat with the other comics before hitting the stage. The next night I got to the club early and while talking with the feature act, we got on the subject of how I wanted to get into the convention market and also about how about comics screw you over. I mentioned that the only reason I was doing this emcee gig was that the emcee at the last gig pulled a dirty trick by doing three stupid car jokes and then bringing me out to a cold audience. As I'm saying that, I realized that I'd heard those same stupid car jokes *the night before from him*! I blurted out, "It's you! You screwed me over!" I then went on a rant yelling at him and telling him basically what an awful thing he'd done and what a lousy way that was to treat someone. And he agreed! He said the club owner even said something to him about it the night it happened. But he did get bumped up to feature!

He felt really bad and apologized profusely. But he took it one step further. He picked up the phone right then and made a bunch of calls on my behalf. He called his agent and got me an audition for colleges; he called a major club I had been trying to get into and got me an audition; and he called his friend Frank King. Frank was already working in the convention market, so he asked Frank if he'd talk to me and give me some advice for getting into it. To his credit, this comic worked really hard to make amends right there on the spot.

Accidental Timing

I did end up speaking with Frank, and I acknowledged that I wasn't ready for the convention market yet. Frank gave me some great advice for the future, and years later when I was ready to get into conventions, Frank was a key in helping me.

So I continued working the road in clubs for a couple more years until another serendipitous event happened. I called a comedy club to set up a showcase, and the guy who answered the phone, said that he and his business partner had split; his partner got the comedy club and he got the phone number and the convention business. He asked if I had a clean act and if I wanted to do convention work because he was looking for a female comedian. I said yes, yes, yes! And so every December for the next three years, he booked me to do all sorts of company holiday events. I cut my teeth doing convention work because of that phone call.

Tampering with the Tape

Going from comedy clubs to conventions involved some luck, but I also had to intentionally pursue it. Once I got to Los Angeles, I was doing those holiday events, and I had reconnected with Frank King, who was showing me the ropes of convention work. But I realized I needed a different video tape.

Comedy club owners wanted to see a 45-minute tape, so they felt comfortable that you had 45 minutes of material. Convention clients didn't want to watch a whole tape, but they did want to know that you have done convention work before. So the new tape I put together included testimonials, lists of companies and professional groups I'd performed for, a narrator, as well as a sampling of my convention performances. I found a great video editor who put it all together, and then I duplicated it on VHS (the latest and greatest technology at the time) and sent copies to several agents. My first feedback was awful. An agent you'll read about in the last chapter, the one who had tried to get me to fail, called to tell me that the audio quality wasn't good enough for meeting planners. I feel like that guy took pleasure in telling me I had a crappy tape, although, as it turned out, giving me that feedback was the only nice thing he ever did for me.

I once worked with a woman who dressed very sexy: high heels, short skirt, you get the picture. Her act was terrible. I worked with her again three years later, and her act was great but she was wearing jeans and a tee-shirt. I asked her about the change in clothing, and she blushed and said, "I wore those tight outfits in the hopes that no one would notice how bad my material was and that I didn't have enough material." Personally, I've always written jokes to cover the time. I didn't realize dressing sexy was an option.

But there was no way around it. I had to redo the tape quickly. I was panicked. I was flat broke. This tape had cost me a lot of money, and I needed it to pay off with some bookings. Ramen noodles were a pretty steady diet, and I was already cutting out expensive foods like asparagus. I needed to buy some fresh fruit before scurvy set in and I'd have to write some "if I had my teeth" jokes.

Luckily, that next week I was already booked at the D.C. Improv, my home club. I called my buddy Rob, and he calmed me down by saying he would bring his video equipment so I could get a quality tape. Now all I had to do was have a great show. Nothing like pressure to make for a stressful event! But the audience laughed and I was I relieved!

Rob produced a great tape for me that had fantastic video and audio; the editor needed another $300 to slip these bits into the tape, and I was set. I checked my bank account and had exactly $300. I remember my hand was shaking as I pulled the rest of my savings out of the ATM. I thought, "This is it. I have to book some work off this tape or become a waitress. Or move back east. Or stay in the clubs and waitress." I got the tape edited and, with some help from Frank, I sent it out to an even bigger list of agents and meeting planners. I braced myself for more feedback. And I got it. Off of that one mailing, I booked $30,000 worth of work. Whew! I could put the waitress application away and continue as a comedian.

Customizing for Convention Work

When I got into doing shows for convention events, I still had another issue. I know, some days I wondered if this ever gets easier! The problem now was that I'd been working the clubs really hard, and while I didn't have a dirty act in which I cursed and spoke graphically about body parts, there were certainly some jokes that just weren't right for a business crowd. They still crack me up, but I just couldn't say 'em to an audience all dressed up at a banquet. Jokes like: I knew it was time to lose weight when I went to have my annual exam at Planned Parenthood. They had protesters out front, and one of 'em grabbed me and screamed, "You can't go in; you're too far along!" I yelled back, "I'm not pregnant. I'm bloated." It's a funny joke but just not right for dinner guests. So I had this 15-minute gap in my 60-minute set. Did that stop me from marketing and accepting convention work? No way. I decided that since I'm a good, and more importantly FAST, joke writer (See my first book *Finding the Funny Fast: How to Create Quick Humor to Connect with Clients, Coworkers and Crowds.*), that I'd kick off my show with jokes about the group and their event.

That decision turned out to be a blast! I did a ton of research on the groups I was performing for, and I learned a lot about them and their industries. I then developed some great material to kick off each show and connect immediately to the audience. Unknowingly, I opened up a fantastic niche for myself and built a fabulous reputation for tailoring my act to the event. Sometimes the jokes I wrote for the group were so good, that my act had a hard time following them! The audience would be like, "Hey, we're talking about us. Why are you changing gears and talking about you? Keep talking about us, us, us!"

My leap into the convention market and writing industry-specific material worked beautifully. It has also made my act more interesting to *me* because I love learning about all these different professions.

My career as a convention comedian took off, too, and I'm thrilled to still be doing it today. A few years ago, I ran into the comic with the "three stupid car jokes." He and I had definitely buried the hatchet, and after a few drinks he said, "You know, I made you a lot of money by messing up that audition for you." We both laughed about it. True. But I'm kind of glad he did it!

WISDOM

Allow others to make amends.
People make mistakes and sometimes they sincerely want to make restitution. Don't shut them out if you feel their apology is heartfelt. You never know where it may lead.

Sometimes jerks have a point.
If I had not listened to that agent who I felt had treated me badly, then I would never have made a better quality video tape that resulted in my being booked in the convention market. See if there's a gem of truth in what a jerk is telling you.

Work at your goals consistently.
Some of my luck getting into the convention market was because I worked at my comedy career goals consistently. The showcasing and phone calls led to the convention connections.

Push yourself if you are willing to do the work.
If you are willing to put 100 percent into something new, like I was in writing company-specific jokes to break into a new market, then do it and see where it takes you.

chapter eleven

Fame and the Famous

I'm a comedian, and friends, family and prospective clients always want to know how famous I am. I've been rejected for gigs because the client wanted "someone who's been on TV." That's a shame because many of us very good comedians have not had our national five minutes of fame. And while being in the media can be a stamp of approval from the industry, it doesn't necessarily mean that the comic is the best choice for the client's event. A comic might have a great agent who got him there or her dad might be president of the network. It also doesn't mean that they're making a living at comedy. I've seen comics on TV who also had "day jobs" (think Target) to pay their bills. I've decided fame will get you 10 minutes. If you're famous, you can bomb onstage for 10 minutes before the audience gets mad at you. They've already decided that you're funny because you're famous. But if you bomb more than 10 minutes, the audience is furious because they've paid a lot more money to see you.

Those of us who aren't famous have about 60 seconds to prove we are funny before the audience turns on us. And if you're hiring a famous comedian, keep in mind that you pay a lot more and you can't tell them what to do. If they curse in their act, just know that they will curse at your convention. Many of the stories in this book wouldn't happen to famous comedians because they can put their foot down when it comes to spinning rooms (Chapter 3) and drunken attendees (Chapter 7).

Oprah Smoprah and Other Credits

I once got within a hair of appearing on "The Oprah Winfrey Show." My friend Rob had a buddy who worked there, and they were doing a comedy segment in which they were taking an ordinary person and having a famous comedian work with him for a short time. The crowning event would be a showcase at a comedy club for the ordinary person, where they would tape his set and then interview him on Oprah's show.

I came in because they were looking for a working but unknown comedian whose act they could compare the new person's. Both videos would be shown back to back on "The Oprah Winfrey Show," and the audience would vote which person was the "real" comedian. Not being a celebrity finally worked in my favor! I even had a gig in Chicago the week they were taping the show, so I could be on the show too. Some of my friends thought I was nuts because what if the audience didn't pick me as the real comedian? Wouldn't that make me look bad? Are you kidding? I would get national exposure on Oprah's show!

Rob's friend called me and I was all set to go except one tiny, overlooked fact: You cannot become a comedian in a few short weeks. This became apparent when the newbie went onstage. Rob called me after the new person performed his showcase and gave me a heads up that, in his opinion, they could not put my tape next to this person's because it would be no contest. He said that aside from messing up material, the newbie had no stage presence. Stage presence is what you get from the good, the bad and the mediocre gigs; you can't rush this process. And as Rob predicted, the producer called me the next day. He was very nice but said they had changed the segment and wouldn't need me. I was crushed that I wouldn't get my shot on TV but a little pleased that someone couldn't waltz in and become a comedian overnight.

A lot of people think they can become comedians instantly because they're funny with their friends. They come up after the show to tell me how they should be a comedian because they are *hilarious*. Good, go do it, but just know that the easier it looks onstage, the harder we have worked. Some sitcom stars who are actors, not comedians, will try to make some extra money doing comedy when the show is on hiatus. Sometimes they get themselves in trouble though because they go onstage at a comedy club and try to follow comics who do this every week for a living. The guy or girl working the comedy road usually buries them, and about 10 minutes in, the sitcom star is lost and the audience is disappointed. You just can't get onstage and instantly be funny for 45 minutes. In comedy, like most jobs, you have to start at the bottom of the ladder.

Tiny Stabs at Fame

I haven't really tried hard to be famous, but I have done a few things. I won an HBO comedy contest back when I lived in D.C. That sounds impressive except that it was held in the middle of a mall. Sure, a friend and I were flown out to the taping of HBO's "Comic Relief" and treated royally. And I got a comedy credit with the word "HBO" in it. But I told jokes on a stage in a mall to an audience of people who were there mostly to visit Sears or Macy's. In fact, some of the people in the competition started out as shoppers! I didn't even know about the contest. I just happened to be exercising with my Sony Walkman (I'm dating myself) when I heard a radio announcement that the contest would start in an hour. Have you ever been in a place where you just *knew* you were supposed to be someplace else? It felt like a universal force pushing me, and I had this huge urgency to get over to that mall. I can't explain it, but I just did, so I Walkmanned myself on over there.

The contest consisted of each entrant telling a joke, and the worst one was voted off. The remaining contestants then told another and so on. A comic friend, Dave, was already signed up, and he shared his strategy with me; do your best joke first and weed out the shoppers! We did about eight rounds of round-robin-joke-telling until it was down to just Dave and me. His strategy worked. Even better, thankfully, I wasn't beaten out by a shopper; that would've been a lot more embarrassing than losing on "The Oprah Winfrey Show." In the last round, Dave told a very funny but mean joke about his little sister. The crowd turned on him. I did my killer closing joke and won! The trip to Los Angeles was fun, though it didn't get me anywhere except front row seats to watch other comics tape an HBO Comic Relief special.

I also got an audition on "Last Comic Standing." What I learned: Don't do work jokes late at night. No one wants to think about work. And speaking of work, I'm one of the few comics whose credits include *The Wall Street Journal* and *The Washington Post*. The only heads up I had that I might be included in a *WSJ* article was when I got a call from a secretary at an entertainment agency who asked for a link to my website. She had no details about the article, so I had no idea it was happening until the next morning when my dad called really early. I thought it was a family emergency, but it turned out he had opened the paper and saw me featured in that article. I think he was finally on board with my career choice then! I was also featured in *The Washington Post*. Gene Weingarten tossed out a challenge to a few of us "clean comics" to write clean punchlines to traditionally dirty joke set-ups, such as "There once was a girl from Nantucket . . . ." I got a few good jokes in and another weird credit.

Being Around Famous People

Every July the Comedy & Magic Club in Hermosa Beach, California, celebrates its birthday by having 20 or so comics come in each night and do four minutes of material. This is the club where Jay Leno performs every Sunday night, and they've been super nice to me. The celebration is a lot of fun and I get to work with comedians I've known from the road as well as famous acts. I've had to follow comics such as Garry Shandling and Michael Richards, the guy who played Kramer on "Seinfeld." (This was prior to all his bad press.) At that time, Richards was walking onstage to standing ovations even before he opened his mouth. And he followed it with funny, so he was a really hard act to follow. When I stepped onstage, it was like, "Who the heck is Jan McInnis?" So I opened with "Didn't you all love him as Kramer on 'Seinfeld'? He was so goofy. He reminds me of every blind date I've ever been on." It got a good laugh and offered the audience a way to cross over to me.

If people realized how easy it is to walk into green rooms, they'd do it. I once performed in Vegas right after the "Thunder from Down Under" male stripper show. One thousand women were screaming for them during their show. Afterwards, I just opened the door next to the stage and walked into the green room. The guys were in various stages of undress, and they said, "Hey, who are you?" I said, "I'm the comedian on the next show." They just turned back to getting dressed with an "Oh, ok." Three magic words "I'm the comedian" will open doors!

Another famous comedian I worked with, aside from Larry the Cable Guy, whom I mentioned in Chapter 6, was

Jon Stewart. We were at The Punchline comedy club in Atlanta. It was right after he took over "The Daily Show," and it was the first time I truly saw "star power." Jon and another comedian and I went to see the movie "The Mummy" Saturday afternoon, and I was amazed to see people's heads snapping as Jon walked through the theater. Of course, maybe it was me they were looking at and wondering, "Is that 'the working girl'?" OK, maybe not.

I saw this kind of star power again when I was headlining for a week in a comedy club and they brought in a soap opera star to headline one show. The room was packed with women who were in awe of him, and after his show, a huge line of women was waiting for his autograph. Magic Johnson would've been envious. The second show that night, I was back to headlining, but I guess the word didn't make it to everyone. A table full of women glared at me as I started my show, and halfway through, they walked out. Turns out it was a bridal shower, and they thought the soap star would be on the second show, too. I guess they didn't notice the ticket price difference.

I once had a day in which I got rejection letters from two comedy clubs and a late-night TV show. I just went to bed. I ended up getting into both of those clubs eventually but not the TV show.

I also opened for Julio Iglesias. He's such a huge star that you'd think his opening act would be given the five-star treatment too. Well, I got there early for the sound check, but nobody really cared. I couldn't get anyone to do a sound check. I also had to share a dressing room with a dozen or so 20-something dancing girls, and there were a bunch of water bottles on a piano backstage, but they wouldn't let me have one because they were "Julio's water." A microphone was a little hard to track down too;

about a minute before I went onstage someone handed me one, and then I was sent out with no introduction. I felt like I wasn't there to warm up the audience so much as to settle them down. Waiters were still walking by and people were still being seated. I took the gig because it was last-minute and I thought it would be a fun credit. Not so much. My friend Mary attended, but she got thrown out for taking my picture, though she still got some great shots. She tried to pass herself off as my PR person, and as they were tossing her out the door, she yelled, "Jan will never perform for Julio again!" And she was right, though I'm sure it's mutual between Julio and me. The only Julio interaction I had was saying hi to him as I walked off and he went on. I didn't stay for the show, and there's a chance that I grabbed a bottle of "Julio's water" as I headed to a bar down the street. So much for opening for big names.

And while I've never had the pleasure of meeting Ellen DeGeneres, I did get to imitate her once. I got an email from an agent saying his client was working on the movie "Finding Nemo." They wanted a female comedian who could sound like Ellen and who had great comedic timing to do some "pick up" lines of hers so she didn't have to come back into the studio. How fun! They sent me a clip of her lines so I could practice, but unfortunately I didn't see the email until the day before the audition, so I didn't have much time. I got into the Disney studio, which was cool, and I was able to mimic her lines pretty well when they played them. The studio engineers and the client were cracking up, but the purpose was for me to do lines that she *didn't* say, so they could insert them; I wasn't good enough at that, so a great opportunity went away. A few months later, when the movie came out, my five-year-old niece piped up with, "Isn't that the movie you tried out for but didn't get?" Yeah, thanks for keeping score.

Speaking of imitating people, I have been, and perhaps may again be, a Hillary Clinton impersonator. Impersonators are different from imposters because an impersonator doesn't have to "come clean" and go back to her own persona. We stay in character for the whole gig, and I actually enjoyed being someone else. An agent encouraged me to be Hillary when he noted that there were no comedian Hillarys, just meet-and-greet Hillarys. My comedian buddy Frank King became my Bill, and we did a few gigs together before Hillary ended all of our dreams by dropping out of the 2008 presidential race!

To be Hillary, I had to wear a facial prosthetic, and trust me, it is not like those "Mission Impossible" movies where they peel it on and off in seconds. If they showed the real process, that movie would've been about 18 hours long! First, a makeup artist creates a mold of your face by covering your face in plaster. My claustrophobia kicked in big time and I made the makeup artist talk to me the entire 45 minutes. Then, every time I wanted to be Hillary, he had to fill the mold with a liquid plastic and let it gel overnight. It then takes about two hours to apply the mask, along with appropriate Hillary makeup. I add a wig and conservative pantsuit, and ta-da! I am Hillary.

Frank and I did an all-day event once in which my "face" kept peeling off. The gig was pretty grueling, as our clients wanted us to run around the convention center and drum up interest in their product. Bill pretended to hit on all the women and I would yell at him. We were sort of an annoying Bill and Hillary team.

I've also worked at a club on the Vegas strip with my name on the marquee in lights. This made me feel like a big star; however, ironically, the first time I worked there, I was so broke I couldn't afford a camera to take a picture of my face and name in lights! Luckily, the booker had a camera.

Fame Behind the Scenes

I like living in Los Angeles and being around the entertainment industry, but as entertainers, we have to be careful or we can start feeling really bad about our careers. When I first moved here, I hung out at the L.A. Improv a lot with my comedian friends, and one night in particular I was getting more and more depressed as it seemed like everyone had "a deal" but me. I was doing well working comedy clubs and selling jokes to radio and TV, but I didn't have any development offers pending or sitcom producers banging on my door. As I drove home that night, I was pretty down until I walked into my studio apartment, turned on the TV and saw Jay Leno, saying one of the jokes I had faxed in that day. Yippee! That reminded me that I really did have a few things going for me. Unfortunately, the only one I could brag to about it that night was my cat.

Another time I was at the Improv, one of the few agents who ever talked to me pulled me over and excitedly declared, "You made the list!" I asked what list and she said, "The list of about 20 comedians being considered for female comedian of the year at the comedy awards." I don't know which club nominated me, but I was flattered even though I never heard anything else about it.

And I've been on radio a lot. I had a short-lived radio project titled "Cubicle Comedy with the Work Lady" in which I did a weekly five-minute radio spot offering funny work advice. It didn't really go anywhere, and I ended up putting some of the advice on playing cards that I now sell as "Cubicle Comedy Playing Cards."

I've also written comedy for radio and TV, which I detail in my book *Finding the Funny Fast: How to Create Quick Humor to Connect with Clients, Coworkers and Crowds*. I won't list them here, but I've done some neat writing projects.

WISDOM

Being famous isn't important . . . *to me*.
Figure out what aspect of a goal you really want. I started out thinking I must have a major TV credit to make a living at comedy, but I eventually decided that what I really wanted was a comedy career that allowed me freedom in my personal life and not being gone so many weeks on the road. Turns out I could get that without TV credits and not having them has never affected me.

We all have something working for us.
It may not be what everyone else has, but it might turn out to be more unique. A newspaper article instead of a TV show at least helps you stand out from the crowd.

Do something unconventional.
Don't do something the way everyone else is doing it. When I started out, the standard formula for comedy success was work comedy clubs, get an agent, get a TV spot or two and get well known so you can make more money. The problem was the comedy boom had passed, and there were so many comedians on late-night TV shows that doing them didn't make you a star. I had to come up with a different way to make a good living at this, so I focused on the lesser-known convention market.

chapter twelve

Weird Gigs to Support My Comedy

Occasionally I've done work in the entertainment business that isn't comedy but that supports my comedy career. And, no, I'm not talking about dancing around a pole. As I understand it, those jobs are just for girls "putting themselves through school."

Extra Weird Extra Work

When I first moved to Los Angeles, I did "extra" work on TV shows, movies and commercials. Extras are needed to walk around in the background on the set to make the scene look busy and come alive, hence, the term "extras." On my first day on a set, someone burst my bubble and told me, "We are just props that eat." True, but there are people who make their entire living as extras, and if you watch TV, especially commercials, you'll see some of the same people roaming around in the background.

The extra work I did didn't pay particularly well since I was nonunion, but the work was a good fit for me because I spent most of the time sitting around waiting to go on.

All this hanging out meant I could make phone calls and write jokes. Plus I figured extra work was a good gig because when I became a big star, I'd know something about TV and movie shoots so I wouldn't embarrass myself. Though now it's been so long since I did this work that I've probably forgotten everything I learned and/or they've changed procedures, so I'll probably embarrass myself anyway when I get to that level.

To get extra work, you signed up with an "extras" agency and then every night you called a phone number to hear a recording that would make the ACLU cringe. Since these shows and commercials are looking for specific types of people, they get really specific about what they're asking for. The recording

I get all sorts of weird requests. Someone once sent me an email asking if I'd donate a bra for charity. That was either a funny way to raise money or a brilliant way to collect bras for your fetish. Not knowing the guy, I declined.

And as a Hillary Clinton impersonator, I was once asked if I would dress up with my Hillary prosthetic face and wig, but instead of the conservative business suit, the client wanted me to wear leather and carry a whip. Let's see, on the one hand, no one will know who I am. On the other hand I will have to live with myself forever after doing that! I declined, but sadly only after I asked how much money. The right amount buys a lot of therapy.

goes something like, "OK, tomorrow, we're looking for fat people. We need really big, fat, obese people who are overweight by at least 80 pounds," or "We need white males age 18 who look 12" or "We need tall, black women over 40." You get the picture, they want a certain look, and if you fit the bill, you call another number and get booked. You then have to show up at some horrible hour like 3 a.m., well before the rest of the cast. Because extras are notorious for being unreliable, they want you there early. You also have to bring your own outfits (at least three) so the costume woman can go through your clothes and insult your taste. Though she'll eventually find something that works. I once had a woman tell me my clothing didn't look very nice, and I was playing a homeless person!

A perk of extra work was that they fed you on the sets. Albeit, we nonunion workers, on a few occasions, were treated differently than the union extras; they'd have separate tables with nice food for union and PB&J for nonunion. And I remember on one set, there were only four union extras, and the rest of us were nonunion, so the four union people took yellow police tape and marked off an area around their chairs so that we nonunion types couldn't cross over into their forbidden land. Apartheid was alive and well on that set.

I did get some cool gigs doing this extra work though. My mom got really excited once when I spent an entire episode of "Ally McBeal" sitting behind Calista Flockhart in court. Mom broadcast my "success" to friends and family so they could watch the episode. I've had my name in lights on the Vegas strip, sold jokes to late-night TV and performed in front of thousands of people every week. But give me a (very) few bucks to sit behind Calista, and I'm a star!

I also got to be in the first "Charlie's Angels" movie with Lucy Liu, Cameron Diaz and Drew Barrymore, and it was the day that all the stars were on the set. I was in a race track scene. If you look closely and put the movie on pause, you might see me in my smart green pantsuit strolling around the infield. I won't tell you which one of those ladies flashed us extras by pulling up her shirt, but I guess she felt sorry for us. I wasn't impressed by the star-flashing, but the coolest part for me was getting sunburned because the next day I got to sit in the makeup trailer to get my red face toned down. And sitting next to me was Tim Curry of "The Rocky Horry Picture Show" fame. He, I and the makeup lady had a nice chat, and she kept us entertained with stories about doing makeup on Farah Fawcett for the original "Charlie's Angels" TV show!

One thing I forgot to mention, before you start thinking that this is a cool way to make a living, is that extra work is full of crazies. I mean really crazy people. The studios, at least when I was doing it, didn't do any kind of background checks, so lots of people fresh out of prison did extra work. And when it's a big scene requiring hundreds of people, they will take *anyone*. I did a movie at a large events center in Los Angeles with hundreds of extras, and I had to plaster my purse to my side because I was surrounded by nut jobs. After the first scene, they told us to move around and switch places so we'd look like a different group. I decided I was going up to the top of the bleachers, as far away as I could get from everyone. As I'm climbing up there, I hear someone yelling, "Jan, Jan, Jan!" I look up and it's my buddy David, whom I had met on a set earlier that month. Ah, a normal person! We must have looked like that commercial where the couple is running through a field toward each other until they meet and embrace. He had the exact same experience as I did with whackos, so he had headed for the rafters too. For the rest of the day, even when they told us to sit with new people, David and I would not leave each other's sides.

And speaking of nutty people, I was an extra on a right-wing TV talk show featuring a very unpopular, opinionated (in my opinion) person. I'm guessing it was unpopular because the network had to pay people to be in the audience of this short-lived program. Perhaps no one would do it for free? There were crazies there, too, and I'm not just talking about the host. We had to reshoot an entire bit because one of the extras in the front row fell asleep (or passed out). Considering what he was wearing, I'm guessing the latter. They made me sit in front, and three times the producers approached me asking if I would stand up and ask a question they had written, you know, like I was a fan and needed advice. I declined, saying, "I'm only here for the money. I don't agree with the views." I think they were searching for decently dressed, literate people. I must not have worn my "homeless" person outfit that day.

I did this extra work on and off for a couple of years, and I racked up a slew of TV shows like "Boston Legal," "Gilmore Girls," "ER" and others that are long gone. And I got on some made-for-TV movies like the one about the Billie Jean King versus Bobby Riggs tennis match.

Commercials were actually more interesting to me though. The pay was a little better and the shoots seemed to go faster than for TV shows. I got national attention on a couple commercials I did for movies in which the studios paid us to say nice things about their newly released move, a movie we didn't get to watch. I did one of these once, and then went back a week later to do a different movie. The director said, "Hey, I remember you. You can't do this again." I said, "Please, I need the money." He relented and paired me up with a guy and some kids so I would look different. Don't you know? *That's* the commercial that my friends back home saw. I got a few calls asking if I had gotten married in the six months since I moved to Los Angeles. I think the studios got a little flak for doing this fake movie review thing, so this type of extra work came and went pretty quickly.

> *My comedian friend, Michael, and I used to run a showcase in Los Angeles for us as well as others to get stage time. The comedians weren't really big names, but we once got visited by Sally Struthers, of "All in the Family" fame, and LeAnn Rimes. There were only about 20 people in the audience, and Sally's voice was very recognizable!*

Though it was interesting, I can't say I liked extra work much because you were told when you could take breaks. They also kept you in the dark about the agenda for the day, so you had no idea how long the shoot would run. I would get bored and wander away from our holding pen only to have to slip in while they were shooting a scene. Continuity is a big thing in the TV/movie business and they don't like having an extra behind the actor one minute and gone the next. I never got caught, but I'm sure I screwed up a few shots. My wanderings led me to some great conversations though. I once ended up talking with one of the crew who used to be a roadie for Willie Nelson. That was more interesting than watching the union extras wrap police tape around themselves.

I once found myself sitting in a factory surrounded by women from other countries who are fast at work on their sewing machines making stripper clothing. Yes, clothing for strippers. I couldn't talk with these women because of the language barrier, but I'm sure they wondered what a tall, gawky-looking girl like me was doing there. They probably figured I was the bottom of the barrel when it comes to dancers—maybe a dollar-store dancer or something. That was many years ago, and I happened to be there not because I was looking for new outfits for the stage but because I had a day off between comedy club gigs and I was staying with a friend who had a line of stripper clothing. I could hang out in his factory and use the Internet all day for free (in the days of dial-up).

Five Minutes of Fame: Showcases, Competitions and Guest Sets

One of the staples of life as a comedian is doing showcases, competitions and guest sets. These don't really pay, but they are another way we build our careers because people get to see us, and then maybe they'll hire us. This is the reason that some (not all) comedy clubs in major cities like New York and Los Angeles pay only a small fee to the performers for a set. It's a privilege to get on their stage because you might be "discovered"!

Showcases occur when you're trying to get work and the client or club owner wants to see a few minutes of your act. I've done these to get both comedy club work and convention work, and for the most part I've done well in showcases thanks to my setup punch jokes. I do three or four jokes a minute, so in five minutes I can cram in 20 short jokes and give people a nice sample of my act.

But sometimes showcases are not so helpful because the person who is supposed to see you doesn't show up. I once showcased at a club during my move cross-country to Los Angeles. I had set it up in advance and had a killer showcase, only to find out that the club owner never came in to see me. I let it go and continued my move. About six months later, I'm standing at the bar in the famous Improv on Melrose Avenue in Los Angeles, and this guy I've never seen before yells, "Jan McInnis! How are you?" I looked at him and he said his name. Turns out that he was the club owner from the aforementioned club. He recognized me from my headshot (thankfully, I look like my picture) and he went on to rave about how his waitstaff raved about me and my act. He said to call him on Wednesday nights at 8 o'clock because that's when he does his booking. I was flattered and stunned. He seemed sincere and there was really no reason for him to acknowledge me, since I had no idea what he looked like. Of course, flattered and stunned turned to frustrated and irritated after I tried for four solid years, calling almost every single Wednesday night at 8, to get a booking. I never did.

Aside from showcases, there are comedy competitions. These have gotten publicity due to the TV show "The Last Comic Standing," but they've been around for a long time. I've entered a few, and have usually done well. I once got on one because I happened to be in town when they were running a contest. The organizer slipped me into the opening slot, and I killed; I had a *great* set. The rest of the contestants followed me and there was only one person who even came close to what I did. So everyone figured I was going to at least place. When we all filed in to hear the results, the entire room was staring at me; pretty cool, except that I didn't even place! The woman who came close to my set won, and the second place went to a woman who had stormed out of the room in tears because she had such a bad set.

Afterward, I was swarmed by people who wanted to know what happened. Because I went on first, did I get lower scores until they realized that mine should have been higher? I had no idea, but I did notice that one of the judges was a comedy club owner who didn't like me personally. I'd had a run-in with him because of an idea that I had and he wanted to "borrow." I didn't let him have it, and he was pissed. Oh, well, I guess he got me back.

Guest sets are similar to showcases, but in these cases you're already in with the club, and you're just dropping in to get a few minutes of stage time, sometimes to try out new material. If you're attending a club and Jerry Seinfeld isn't on the show, but he does five minutes, then he's doing a guest set. It's a courtesy to let a comic, regardless of fame, do a few minutes on the show. But unless you're famous, you really need to call and arrange it with the club owner first. Seinfeld can just pop by. I think most comedians are polite about it and just do their time, but sometimes famous people will go over their time, which I think is rude. I was scheduled for a showcase one night, so I could get into a big club, and a famous comedian popped in to do a guest set. As a courtesy, the club let him on, and he proceeded to do 30 or 40 minutes instead of five. He ate up my time and I never got to showcase.

All of these weird gigs have given me a well-rounded and fun experience in the entertainment industry.

WISDOM

You never know who's watching.
Sometimes the obvious person, like the club owner at the showcase, who is supposed to watch doesn't, but the wait staff does, and they still count. You never know who can help or hurt your efforts.

Make good use of your time.
Don't be afraid to take on a weird gig if it supports your efforts to reach your goals. Get creative and have fun on the journey.

chapter thirteen

And Finally . . .

I've got one last story for you. This book began with me, early in my comedy club career, in front of 200 slightly inebriated coal miners, and I bombed horribly. Fast forward eight years, I'm backstage waiting to go on in front of 1,500 people, my biggest crowd ever. It was also my first big convention gig. I'd been talking with Frank King about convention work, and he was on this show too, so I was excited to finally meet him in person. If all goes well and my act hits big, I'm hoping he'll like it and help me get into more convention work. I was feeling a little pressure.

Then in walks the other comedian on the show. He and I recognized each other immediately; he was the high-energy emcee from six years earlier, when I worked at his home club and he had all those local references. It was the same club where I pulled out a fistful of comment cards and they all said they hated me. I'm sure he thought I was a horrible comic. The pressure ratcheted up a notch.

And finally, the other player that night was the agent. I'd never met him before, and I had the impression that he did not really want me on this show, that he had booked me as a favor to a friend, and I could just tell that I was not his first choice.

I looked out at the 1,500 people and realized this was not my crowd: Mostly guys, mostly more than "slightly inebriated," and mostly good ole boys. I looked at Frank and said, "I may have to say some jokes that aren't 'convention-friendly' to get through this. I hope you understand." He looked at me and said, "Me, too."

And to top things off, this was a variety show format, and so while I was the first comic up, I was following some sort of dancing girl act. Yeah, 1,500 drunk guys watching a dozen dancing girls, and then me. One of my first big convention shows seemed to have all the makings of my hard bar gigs, but with more people. The pressure just kept building.

As it neared "go time," my knees got that familiar shaky feeling and I started to sweat. Then as they began announcing me, the agent leans over and whispers in my ear, "Women never do well at this event." The next words I heard were, "Welcome comedian Jan McInnis."

I strolled out, with one comic thinking I stink, one comic who could possibly help me get into convention work, an agent who, in my opinion, just tried to sabotage my show and 1,500 drunk guys in front of me. Oh, and I was following dancing girls!

I went into my first joke . . . and it hit big! From the first punch line, I had these people, and I kept at them, doing it with my clean material, never having to do any "not-convention-friendly" material. It was fun! I walked offstage to thunderous applause and even more relief. Whew! The comic who had seen me bomb at the sister clubs went up next and he struggled for the first few minutes. They weren't buying the high energy at first but then he got them going. To his credit, he came to me after his set and acknowledged that at one point he wasn't sure he was going to be able to follow me. Frank, of course, did great, and the show was a hit.

Afterwards at the VIP party, it was flattering to walk into the room and have heads turn and a path part for us as we walked through. People were really complimentary—all except that agent. When I asked if he might be interested in putting me on his roster, he said he'd think about it. The only other time I heard from him was when he told me that my first corporate tape was awful (mentioned back in Chapter 10). But I didn't care because my convention comedy career was off and running and I couldn't have been happier.

I end with this story because it's a great example of what has happened to me throughout my comedy career. Things have always worked out, usually to my advantage, maybe not the way I had originally intended, but they did. My mom used to say, "Everything always works out," and I truly believe it. I just had to stick with it long enough to see how the pieces fit together.

Wrapping It Up

I hope this book has entertained you, given you some insight into a job you'll never do (or never want to do!) and maybe even inspired you to move forward with whatever project it is that's been gnawing at you. I'm not really trying to be a motivational speaker here. I've only been called that once, when my sister was adopting her kids. She told me that on the form for the home study, where they ask all about relatives, she didn't want to put my profession as "comedian" because it sounded too "sketchy." So she wrote that I was a motivational speaker, and she asked me to confirm that with the home study woman if she called. I still haven't forgiven her for that! But I put off getting into stand-up comedy for a long time, and I would encourage you not to wait so long if there is something burning you up inside that you need to do. If you wait, the only thing that changes is your age.

These are just a few of the stories I have, the ones that stick out and that I believe really taught me something. Everyone has a story about how they got where they are. Thank you for reading mine. And I certainly didn't do all this by myself. I had a tremendous amount of support. There were dozens and dozens of people who helped me along the way, from the comedy club bookers and owners who first took a chance on me to the friends and family who gave me a room to stay in and the people along the way who encouraged me and helped me make connections.

The Next Chapter

I hope to be around in this wonderful, weird business for another 20+ years so I can write the sequel to this book. Although I could stand not having some of the hard gigs and bombing stories, nobody knows what's in store. I've added some more elements to my comedy in the past few years, by doing not just comedy but humorous keynotes. My buddy Frank King introduced me to Kent Rader, who helped me move into this market, and he is one of my true friends in this business. Kent and I have also joined forces to create "The Baby Boomer Comedy Show: Clean Comedy for People Born Before Seatbelts, Safety Helmets and Facebook," which we perform for theatres and convention events throughout the country. My career keeps getting better and more interesting all the time, and just about every day I think to myself that I am the luckiest person on the planet.

And I have to say, through all the bombing, weird gigs, drunks, jerks and travel headaches, it has all worked out and I've enjoyed my job tremendously. In the words of my friend Rob Duffett, "All is well."

Jan

WISDOM

Know why you do what you do.
I'm lucky because I've found my "passion," and experts will tell you that you need to find your passion to be happy. I disagree. That's too much pressure because many people just don't know what their passion is. Instead, I think it's more important that you are crystal clear on why you do what you do, and then make peace with that. Why are you spending your life working at the job you have? Is it just for the money, or because you help people, or maybe the hours are great or you like that particular industry? Every step I took in comedy, whether it was driving on the road, living in a studio apartment or standing in front of drunk conventioneers, I made peace with it in case that was as far as I would ever go in this career. This understanding, to me, is the key to being happy and successful.

About the Author

Jan McInnis has spent the past 20+ years as a comedian, comedy writer and, more recently, as a keynote speaker. She was featured in The Wall Street Journal and The Washington Post for her clean humor, and she has shared her humor with thousands of organizations. She has also sold comedy material to hundreds of radio stations, to greeting cards, websites, a syndicated cartoon strip and late-night TV shows. She is the author of two books and millions of jokes, many of which are in her act and others that she thinks are funny but the audiences didn't.

Born in Washington, D.C., Jan was in charge of the "joke of the day" for her junior high school lunch table. She majored in communications at Virginia Tech, where she was a disk jockey for the local radio station. Jan now resides in Los Angeles.

NOTE

For more information about Jan or to book her for a comedy show or humor keynote, contact her at
www.TheWorkLady.com or Jan@TheWorkLady.com.

Jan's Keynotes:
Cubicle Comedy – clean, hilarious comedy show
Finding the Funny in Change – how to use humor
    to handle change
Finding the Funny in Communications – how to put humor
    into your written and verbal business communications
Hilarious Hosting – great emcee to keep your event rolling

You can also check out her first book, *Finding the Funny Fast: How to Create Quick Humor to Connect with Clients, Coworkers and Crowds* and her "Cubicle Comedy Playing Cards."

Photo by Darwinography

THANK YOU!

All I can say is a THANK YOU to the many, many people who helped make my comedy career possible. Of course, my parents and my siblings have all had a huge part in my success. From the beginning, my mom was excited about my career, and I knew my dad had finally come around when a few years into it, he told me, "Your mom and I want to be your biggest supporters." I've also received lots of help from my family, namely Debbie, Tad, Dan, Robin, Brenda, Glenn, Kathy, Frank, and Christine and their families, who did everything from renting and managing my condo to storing my stuff in their basements to cheering me on from the audience at many events.

There are also tons of other people who encouraged me to become a comedian and who played a huge part in making it happen. Thanks to my friends, extended family, friends of family and family of friends who gave me a place to stay while I was on the road, brought their friends and families out to my shows and always have given me inspiring words along the way to keep me going.

And finally, thanks to the many club owners, bookers, agents and clients who hired me so that I could keep working at this great profession. Some of you booked me when I was just starting out, and I will be forever grateful for you giving me that opportunity.

There are too many people to list who all had a piece in helping me along the way, and I'd probably forget someone, so I have to do this blanket THANK YOU to those who helped me.

I know how fortunate I am to be able to work in a profession that I love, and I am truly grateful to all these wonderful people who have helped make it happen.

CPSIA information can be obtained at www.ICGtesting.com
Printed in the USA
BVOW08s0031240816

459854BV00001B/3/P